THE MYSTERY OF THE
POISON
ARROW TREE

RHINO TALES

SHEL ARENSON

THE MYSTERY OF THE POISON ARROW TREE

Published by Multnomah Youth
a part of the Questar publishing family

© 1996 by Sheldon Arensen
International Standard Book Number: ISBN: 0-88070-899-9

Cover design: Kevin Keller
Cover illustration: Kenneth Spengler

Printed in the United States of America

For information:
QUESTAR PUBLISHERS, INC.
POST OFFICE BOX 1720
SISTERS, OREGON 97759

Library of Congress Cataloging-in-Publication Data

Arensen, Sheldon.
    The mystery of the poison arrow tree / by Shel Arensen.
      p. cm. — (Rhino tales)
    Summary: Members of the Rugendo Rhinos club, a group of American boys
living at a mission station in Kenya, become involved in the strange death of a
village boy and rumors of a deadly curse.
    ISBN 0-88070-899-9 (alk. paper)
    [1. Kenya — Fiction. 2. Clubs — Fiction. 3. Mystery and detective stories.]
I. Title. II. Series.
PZ7.A683My   1996
[Fic] — dc20

96-12312
CIP
AC

96 97 98 99 00 01 02 03 04 05 — 10 9 8 7 6 5 4 3 2 1

To my son, Blake, the original creator of the hot dog car.

THE
GENET CAT
TRAP

"Ouch! I hit a stinging nettle and my leg's on fire!" I complained. Jon and Matt turned from leading the way through the narrow overgrown path. They both scowled at me.

"Pipe down, will you Dean?" Matt commanded in a quiet voice. "You'll scare every animal and bird in the woods."

"Okay, Matt," I whispered. I licked my hand and rubbed it over my nettle sting which was already turning an angry red.

Matt Chadwick gives the commands in our club. That's because he's our club captain. We're the Rugendo Rhinos, four missionary kids who live at Rugendo, a mission station in the highlands of Kenya, Africa. Matt's dad teaches at a Bible school and holds pastors' seminars around the country. Once Matt went with his dad to one of the seminars and got kidnapped, but that's another story.

Jon Freedman motioned for us to follow. Crouching with his air rifle held easily in his hand, he set off again. Jon's our club bush expert. He can track animals through the forest and is our best marksman. He likes to skin animals when our dads take us hunting. Maybe he gets his skill with a knife from his dad, a surgeon and the only doctor at our mission hospital.

Matt always lets Jon lead the way on hikes through the forest. Like today, a Saturday—we'd said good-bye to books for the weekend and were looking for a good place to set our new genet cat trap.

Dave Krenden nudged me from behind with the wooden box in his hand. "Let's go," he whispered. I looked at the box. Dave had made it himself. He loves to build things. He takes after his dad who works as a missionary builder. In fact, Dave designed and almost single-handedly built our tree fort in the huge wild fig tree. We'd all helped, but it was Dave's building ability that had finished the project. The box Dave held now was our genet cat trap. We wanted to see if we could catch a genet cat and then tan the skin.

I motioned for Dave to go ahead as I massaged my sore leg. I'm Dean Sandler. My dad's a writer, and he edits a Christian youth magazine at Rugendo and trains Kenyan writers. I was elected our Rhino club secretary because the others figured if my dad could write, I could too. I really can't. But I manage to scribble enough to keep our club organized.

Sometimes if we've had some really exciting adventure my dad will help me write the story.

The four of us always do everything together even though Matt's in sixth grade, I'm in fifth and Dave and Jon are in fourth grade. That's why we formed our club. And it was Matt's idea to call ourselves the Rugendo Rhinos.

Jon signaled for all of us to stop, and he knelt down behind a low bush. We all huddled up next to him. He pointed silently with his chin the way an African would. Pointing with a finger was not only rude in Africa, in this case it might have scared off the bushbuck Jon spotted at the bottom of the ravine. The wind shifted and a gust from behind us carried our scent to the buck. It tensed, then gave a sharp dog-like bark before bounding away into the forest.

We stood up and stretched. "Beautiful," Matt murmured. "Let's hope there are some genet cats out here too."

Jon said, "Come on. I think we'll find a good place to set our trap under those big trees at the bottom of the ravine."

We slipped our way down the steep bank until we hit the bottom where a small stream trickled during the rainy season. But now, at the height of the dry season, the ravine bottom carried no hint of water.

Jon crouched and began casting about for tracks. Soon he found some small caves on the steep banks above the stream bed with signs that a genet cat had visited recently. He picked up a clump of digested shell-like rings. "Some genet cat has been here eating millipedes," he announced. He held out what was left of a small worm-like creature for us to look at. "Boy, you should see the millipedes on the coast. They get as big as hot dogs, but up here in the high country they stay pretty small." We nodded with respect. Jon liked to pass on his knowledge about animals and bugs.

He pointed out a nearby cedar tree. "I think if we put the trap near the base of that tree we can catch ourselves a genet cat. The tracks show at least one comes by here looking for millipedes to eat. He can't live too far away. So if we set our trap right and bait it well, maybe he'll stop in for a little snack."

Dave took the trap from under his arm and placed it near the tree, like a mother setting her baby down for a nap. The box was about the size of a shoe box only twice as long. He moved the sliding door up and down gently to be sure it would fall correctly. Then he tested the spring mechanism that he'd devised from some wire and a nail. The nail went through a metal curtain ring on top of the door and the wire led from the nail over a small pulley to a bait stick at the far end of the box. If the bait stick was pulled it would jerk the nail out of the door which fell over the entrance and would trap the genet cat. The trap worked perfectly, as Dave's creations always did.

"Now all we have left to do is put some bait on the stick," Matt said, pulling a half-empty jar of rancid peanut butter from his coat pocket.

"Gross!" I said. "The oil leaked all over your coat!"

Matt looked at his oil-soaked coat and then shrugged. "I guess it's my hunting coat from now on." Reaching his finger into the peanut butter, he dug out a large smear. Then he reached into the trap and plastered the bait stick with peanut butter. Dave set the trap carefully while Jon and I gathered leaves and dirt. We covered the trap inside and out to make it look as natural as possible.

When we were finished, we stepped back. Jon broke a small branch from a tree and whisked the area where we'd been standing. Then we eased our way into the forest, arguing about who should check the trap and how often. Since we all wanted to check it first, Matt told us to be quiet. Then he assigned the order in which we would check the trap. He, of course, would be first and would check the trap early the next morning before church.

I asked if we could go by the pond below the hospital on our way back to Rugendo. "My little brother Craig started first grade this year and he wants a jar full of tadpoles for show and tell."

"Sure," Matt said. "You can even use my peanut butter jar. If you carry it, of course." He tossed the greasy jar to me. I caught it and held it an arm's length away from my clothes.

As we got near the pond we heard some goats bleating and tearing at tree leaves. "I wonder who's watching these goats?" asked Dave.

"Looks like a fire over there," Jon said, pointing at smoke coming from behind a bushy tree with red berries growing on it.

Together we came around the tree to investigate what was causing the smoke. And what we saw was a scene I will never forget for the rest of my life!

chapter two

AN UNEXPECTED DISCOVERY!

Two young Kenyan boys lay crumpled on the ground near a smoldering campfire.

"*Jambo! Habari?*" called Matt in a voice that trembled. The boys didn't respond to his greeting.

"Maybe they're sleeping," I said quietly. I could feel my knees shaking, but I didn't want to believe the worst.

"I don't think so," said Jon, edging closer. "Hey, wake up!" His voice sounded strangely loud in the otherwise silent forest.

We could hear ourselves breathing. Dave and I didn't move. It was like my feet were rooted to the ground. Matt and Jon went closer, and Matt tried to turn one of them over, but the boy's arm fell lifelessly into the dust.

"This looks bad," said Matt in a hushed voice, his face pale. Jon kneeled down by the other boy and touched him lightly on the arm. The boy's leg twitched and a low hissing moan eased from his lips, then he drew in a ragged breath of air.

"That's Kamau!" exclaimed Dave when he saw the boy's face. "His dad's a carpentry *fundi*. He works with my dad a lot!"

"Run and get help from the hospital!" Matt was in command now. He looked at Dave and me. "Hurry, you guys! At least Kamau is breathing, we may be able to help him. Jon and I'll stay here—but I don't know what we can do."

"Pray!" exclaimed Jon. That surprised me. He's usually so busy hunting and trapping he doesn't think much about asking God for help. But looking at those two lifeless boys convinced me that prayer was a good idea!

"We'll pray as we run!" I called as I turned and sprinted up the path to the mission hospital. Dave followed right on my heels until I *ran into* a springy branch that had grown over the path. Forgetting my hiking manners, I ran *straight through* and heard the branch smack Dave.

"Ouch!" I heard Dave yell and turned to see him on one knee with his hand over his eyes.

"Are you all right?" I asked, my sides burning.

"I think so, but that branch knocked me in the face and whipped my glasses off."

I quickly examined his face. The branch had left a nasty welt on his forehead. "You've got some scratches, but your eyes seem to be okay."

"But I can't see without my glasses. I can't even find them." He was on his knees scrabbling his fingers through the stiff yellow grass.

I grabbed up his glasses and shoved them back onto his nose.

"We've got to hurry to the hospital. I'll lead the way from here!" exclaimed Dave as he took off ahead of me. I thought of those boys again and panted out another prayer.

A few minutes later we found the hospital chaplain, Pastor Waweru, at the hospital. My heart was pounding and Dave's face was covered with sweat.

"Where's Dr. Freedman?" demanded Dave. "We need to see him right now!"

Pastor Waweru looked surprised. "What's wrong boys? Dr. Freedman is in surgery, but perhaps I can help. Are you hurt?" He looked at the red mark on Dave's forehead.

"No, but two boys are very sick! Maybe even dead!" I blurted breathlessly. "We need Dr. Freedman right away! Can't you please get him?"

"Let's go to the operating theater." Pastor Waweru turned and led us quickly down the corridor. The concrete floor reeked of antiseptic. "You can tell me what you mean as we walk."

"We saw two boys lying on the grass down by the pond," explained Dave. "They looked really sick. One seems to be breathing a little. The other, well, we didn't see him move at all and..."

"We think he's dead," I finished. "And the other boy may be too if we don't get some help soon."

At the operating theater Pastor Waweru sent a nurse in to call Dr. Freedman.

"Do you know who these boys are?" Pastor Waweru asked.

Dave nodded. "The boy who's barely breathing is Kamau, the son of the carpenter who works with my dad, but I don't know the other..."

Pastor Waweru's dark brown face turned charcoal gray. "Kamau is my wife's nephew. He usually herds the goats with Ngugi who is my brother's wife's youngest brother."

Just then Dr. Freedman stepped out of the operating room. He slipped his mask down and smiled. "We saved both the baby and his mom," he announced. "Now, what can I do for you boys?"

Pastor Waweru took him by the hand and pleaded, "Come quick. Two of my young relatives are sick, maybe even dead."

"We found the boys down by the pond," I added. "Matt and Jon are there right now. But the boys need help real bad!"

Dr. Freedman was already in motion. Grabbing his medical bag he began to run, white coat flying out behind him. We had to sprint to catch up. Pastor Waweru called several Kenyan nurses to join us as we raced out of the hospital compound and down the path that led to the pond.

It was about half a mile down to the pond where we'd left Matt and Jon watching over Kamau and his friend. The doctor and Pastor Waweru were already there and kneeling over the two boys by the time Dave and I got there. Dr. Freedman had his head on Kamau's chest. "He's alive, but just barely," he said, more to himself than anyone else. He turned to the other boy.

"It's Ngugi!" cried Pastor Waweru as he recognized the second boy's face.

Dr. Freedman felt for Ngugi's pulse and then listened to the boy's chest with his stethoscope. Looking up he shook his head. "I'm sorry," he announced sadly. "This boy is dead." Then, without waiting for the meaning of his words to hit us, he turned back to Kamau. "And this boy might soon be dead too, if we don't get him to the hospital." He bent down and started to pick up Kamau, and Pastor Waweru quickly stepped in to help, tears glistened on his dark cheeks.

"Bring the other boy, too," Dr. Freedman ordered over his shoulder as the two of them hustled up the path with Kamau. I looked at Matt. His face looked green and I knew mine matched. But before we could do anything the Kenyan nurses picked up the limp body of Ngugi and carried him gently to the hospital.

The four of us followed, not sure what else to do. At the hospital we sat on the white benches in the outpatient lounge, waiting to hear whether Kamau lived or died. Jon scuffed his feet back and forth on the mud-stained cement floor. He always had a hard time sitting still and any kind of waiting was pure agony for him. Finally he stood. "I'm going to find out what's going on from my dad." He turned and marched right into the main part of the hospital.

"Do you think he'll get in trouble?" I asked, concerned that we might get in trouble too.

Matt shrugged. "His dad runs the hospital. He can't get in too much trouble. Besides, I'm getting tired of waiting too. What do you think happened to those two boys anyway? Jon and I looked more closely to see if they'd been shot or some-thing, but we didn't see any blood or wounds or anything unusual."

Just then Jon returned with his dad. Dr. Freedman looked

serious. "Thanks to your quick thinking and getting help, Kamau is alive. But only just. I'd like you boys to pray for him."

"What's wrong with him?" Matt asked the doctor.

"It puzzles me. I have no idea what the sickness is or what could have caused it. Pastor Waweru says both boys were in fine health this morning when they went out to herd the goats. It's a complete mystery. We'll try to do an autopsy on the boy who died. Maybe that will give us some clues. Right now we're doing everything we can to keep Kamau alive. You might as well run along home. There's nothing more you can do."

"There is something," said Pastor Waweru. "We can pray." So we stood in a little circle and asked God to help Kamau to recover, and to be with the families.

As we started to leave the hospital, a large group of Kenyans swarmed through the door. Some of the ladies were wailing with loud penetrating sobs. "Woooi, woooi," they cried in unison. Tears streamed down their faces as they pushed toward Dr. Freedman and Pastor Waweru.

They demanded to know what had happened to the two herd-boys. Pastor Waweru gently explained that Ngugi had died, and that Kamau was alive but very sick. This news was greeted with more wails and tears. We four Rhinos pushed ourselves up against the shiny pink enamel-painted wall, hoping to slip away.

Now the crowd turned to Dr. Freedman. An older man acted as spokesman, and asked what the sickness was. Jon's dad looked over the listening crowd and honestly explained that he didn't know. Then the women, in their brightly printed head scarves, continued to sob and cry.

Pastor Waweru spoke up. "I know this is sad news for everyone. Even I am related to these two boys. But right now Kamau is barely alive. Ngugi is dead. I suggest we come before the Lord in prayer."

Most of the group nodded and the pastor began to pray. "Dear Lord, we come to you with sad hearts today. We don't understand what has happened but we pray—"

"I know what happened," a deep voice interrupted the prayer.

Everyone in the room turned. A large Kenyan man stood in the doorway. His jaw twitched and beads of sweat dripped off his face. He took a step closer and glared at everyone.

"My son Ngugi is dead and I know who is responsible." He took a deep breath and narrowed his eyes. "Baba Kamau, you put a curse on my son!"

Baba Kamau, Kamau's father, looked shocked. "Put a curse on your son? I would never. What do you mean? My son is sick, too—to the point of death. How can you accuse me?"

"You were jealous of my son's success in school," Ngugi's father said. "I know that Kamau's school results were not as good as Ngugi's. You knew that Ngugi would go on to university and help my family out of our poverty. You couldn't stand to see us get ahead. So you went to a witch doctor and cursed my son. Now he's dead!"

Again Baba Kamau tried to protest his innocence, but Ngugi's father acted deaf, as if he'd stuffed two maize cobs in his ears.

"You are going to pay," Ngugi's father shouted, eyes rolling in rage. "I will get my revenge. You cursed my son. I will go to the witch doctor to confirm this and then I will put an even more powerful curse on you and your whole family! Listen, everyone, and remember my words. Calamity will strike the home of Baba Kamau. I have said it!"

Ngugi's father turned and strode out of the hospital. Everyone, including us Rhinos, stood stunned. We had no idea what would happen next.

chapter three

THE SHADOW BY THE POND

The crowd murmured. One wide-hipped woman fainted, her full multi-flowered skirt fluttering down like leaves swirling in the wind. Pastor Waweru moved quickly to help. Jon's dad shook his head; he looked confused. He turned and saw us backed up against the wall.

Frowning, Dr. Freedman said, "You boys get on home. Try to forget what you saw and heard here. Everyone's upset about Ngugi's death right now. They'll go home, plan the funeral and then it'll all be over. You did well to save Kamau's life. Let's pray he doesn't die as well."

Pastor Waweru took Jon's dad aside. He spoke rapidly and earnestly, eyes widening as he talked.

Matt nudged me. "Let's get out of here," he whispered. We crept quietly to the heavy wood and glass doors and escaped into the sunshine. Looking down I noticed I still grasped the greasy peanut butter jar in my hand. "We'd better go back to the pond. I never got the tadpoles for my brother Craig."

"Not me," Matt said, backing away. "I'm not going back there. I don't want to be reminded of Kamau and Ngugi lying on the ground. I'm going home." With that he jogged off.

"I have to go home, too," Jon said, and ran after Matt.

I looked at Dave. "That's strange. I wonder why they won't go back to the pond," he said.

"Maybe staying with the dead boy scared them more than we thought." "You want to join me?"

"Why not?" Dave shrugged, and we set off down the trail.

Back at the pond I wiped off my greasy hands on the stringy grass that grew by the water's edge. Then I scooped the jar full of water. I set it down in the cracked, dried mud along the shore of the pond. Dave and I watched as dirt swirled to the bottom of the jar. When the water cleared we could see two plump tadpoles flicking their tails as they swam.

"All right!" I said. "We got two. Think I should try for some more?"

"Probably not," he advised, with his usual common sense. "You might lose the tadpoles you've already caught."

"I guess you're right. I'd be like the greedy hyena."

"What hyena? I thought we were talking about tadpoles."

"The one in the African folk tale my dad told me last

week. He collects them from African writers during his writing workshops. It goes like this:

"There was this hyena who couldn't find any food. He saw vultures gathering at one lion kill, but by the time he got there, the birds had polished off the meal. Then he tried to join another feast before the lions were finished. They chased him off and warned him to stop crashing their parties. The poor hyena, weak with hunger, stumbled around looking for food.

"Finally, the hyena begged God to give him something to eat. He even promised that if God gave him some meat, he would obey and serve God. Just then the hyena heard the bleating of a goat. With his last bit of strength, the hyena staggered toward the sound. There was a fat goat tied to a tree. By this time he was so starved that he was drooling.

"*I am such a great hunter,* the hyena thought to himself, forgetting his promise to God. *Look at this wonderful goat I've found.*

"God wasn't pleased. Because the hyena acted so proud, God said he would cause the hyena to act foolishly. As the hyena approached the goat, he noticed a cowhide strap tying the goat to the tree.

"*I love to chew on leather,* the hyena thought. *I think I'll eat the strap first as an appetizer before I eat the goat.* So the hyena stepped up and tore through the strap with one bite. But as soon as he did, the goat ran away. The hyena knew he'd made a foolish mistake, but he had no strength left to chase the goat. He laid down and died."

"Quite a story," Dave said. "I really like African stories. I have a hard time listening in church, but I always remember your dad's stories."

As we got up to go, I saw something move behind the bushy tree with the red berries where we'd found the two herd-boys. "What's that over there?" I asked.

Dave looked. "I don't see anything."

"Look, there it is again," I said, pointing this time. "Line up your eyes with that branch on the left. It looks brown and...now it's gone."

"Was it an animal?" Dave stared into the bush.

"I don't think so," I answered. "It was almost like a shadow of a young boy."

Dave looked at me sharply. "You're not seeing ghosts are you?"

"I don't think so. But it was kind of spooky the way it disappeared so suddenly." A chill ran down my back.

"Let's get home," Dave said. "Matt and Jon were right. This place is creepy."

Both of us ran back to Rugendo. All the way the memory of seeing Ngugi dead on the ground scorched an image in my mind.

But as the weeks went by, the memory faded. Kamau recovered, though Jon's dad never figured out what had caused the sickness or why Ngugi died and Kamau didn't. Ngugi's father had angrily claimed his son's body, refusing to let the doctors do an autopsy.

We tried to forget about the tragedy of Ngugi, and we were all thankful that Kamau got well, but school kept us pretty busy. We Rhinos enjoyed school, but we lived for the weekends. It was hard to study when the sun was shining and the nearby forest practically shouted at us to visit.

We almost always played a game of soccer during morning recess. Matt always chose sides and he usually managed to put all of the Rhinos on his team. I played defense, not letting anyone dribble past my long legs. Matt was center forward, scoring goals like crazy. Jon usually swarmed like a bee to wherever the ball was. He once smiled at me when I asked him what position he thought he was playing. "I don't play a position, I just love to kick the ball," he said, and sprinted up the field. Dave played a very careful midfield. Like the center of the old black-and-white clock in our classroom, he rotated in a circle, rarely moving far away from the center of the field. Anytime I got the ball, I tried to kick it to the middle. Dave would calmly step toward the ball, trap it neatly, turn and kick it to Matt.

Even when we played soccer, we'd look up at the forest in the surrounding hills and long for our weekend hikes. But this weekend would be different. It was titchie field day.

At our school, anyone from first to sixth grade was a titchie. I'd learned from my dad that our name came from the British slang word, "titch" meaning anything small or little. We were the little kids at school. We were the titchies. Well, one Saturday each term the titchies had a special games day. There would be races, games and other special events.

Our whole school was divided into two houses or teams. When we first came to the school, we would be assigned to either the Livingstone House or the Stanley House named after the two famous African explorers. Dave and I were Livingstones. And we would always be Livingstones. Matt and Jon were Stanleys. That was the one bad thing about titchie field day. We Rhinos had to play against each other.

During the field day each team would get points for winning games or having runners come in the top three places in races.

The senior store was even more exciting than the games. The twelfth grade class sold doughnuts, candy, hot dogs, and hamburgers. Man, we loved titchie field day. Playing games and eating. And, if we were lucky, we'd find pop bottles that people didn't bother to return to the store. We'd turn them in and get the refund from the seniors, filling our pockets with money to buy more candy.

I always prayed titchie field day would be a sunny day. Who wanted rain to spoil the fun?

The bell signaled the end of recess. I walked off the field with Dave. "Do you think we'll win titchie field day this time?" he asked.

We had both been at the school since first grade and we'd never won titchie field day. The Stanleys had a stranglehold on winning. "I hope so," I said, not sounding very hopeful.

Dave looked at me. "I don't think we have a chance. Jon wins all the races and with Matt on their soccer team they'll win that for sure."

"Some of the Livingstone girls in our fifth grade class are pretty fast," I said. "Maybe they'll win some points."

"Like who?"

"Jill can run faster than most of the boys in fifth grade." *Including me,* I thought but didn't have the courage to say it out loud.

"Are you starting to like Jill?" Dave frowned so his glasses lifted up on his nose.

"Of course not," I said, blushing.

Dave stared at me. "Just wondering. Remember that time you let her join our bike safari? Now you're telling me what a great runner she is."

"We'd better hurry before we're late," I said, hastily

changing the subject. I ran to class before he could say anymore.

chapter four

TITCHIE
FIELD DAY

The morning of titchie field day arrived bright and sunny as prayed for by every titchie in school. The first events were the sprints. As predicted, Jon dominated and won both the fifty- and the hundred-yard dash. After each event, one of the teachers carrying a clipboard would announce the score with a hand-held megaphone. As usual, it looked like a hopeless day for the Livingstones. Then it was time for the girls to race. Dave and I stood to the side to watch. On this day we didn't hang around with Matt and Jon. We saw them on the other side of the soccer field where the races took place.

Jill easily won the fifty-yard dash. "All right, way to go Jill!" I shouted.

Dave raised an eyebrow as he looked at me. "I *thought* you liked her," he said, nodding wisely.

"I'm just cheering for the Livingstones," I said, trying to ignore him. She was tall, like me, and seemed so friendly. I'd never tell Dave, but I did think Jill was kind of cute.

As the teacher read off the score we found that the Livingstones had won all the points in the race. Two new girls from sixth grade had come in second and third. "Hey, we might catch up," Dave said. "I didn't know those two new sixth graders were Livingstones."

As the girls lined up for the hundred-yard dash, Dave started cheering. I couldn't resist getting back at him. "So which one of the two new girls do you like, Dave? You're cheering kind of loud."

"I'm just cheering for the Livingstones," he said. "Like you."

Jill and the two new girls swept the race. "That puts both the Livingstones and Stanleys even," the teacher announced. Dave and I leaped around. Maybe this field day we'd have a chance. We'd never even been close before and now we were tied.

The day went on with high jump and long jump. With a lot of help from the girls, the Livingstones stayed close. I even won third place in the high jump. Not because I jumped very high, but because one of the sixth grade Stanleys banged his knee on the bar and dropped out.

Then came the one event I dreaded. The rope climb. Each titchie had a chance to climb up the rope and win one point for his team. The first time I'd tried this event in first grade I thought it looked so easy. The other kids all scampered up like monkeys. I'd stood on the knot at the bottom of the rope, reached up with both hands and pulled. I expected my body to go up the rope. Nothing happened. I dangled there, horrified at my lack of ability to climb the rope. People had cheered and encouraged but I couldn't move up the rope. Finally I had let go of the rope and hidden behind the crowd, trying to wipe away my embarrassment along with the tears.

Ever since, I'd stayed away from the rope climb. Usually it was late in the day and the Stanleys were so far ahead it made no difference. But today we had a chance. Our winning of the field day could depend on how many Livingstones got up the rope. I decided I couldn't let my team down. I'd at least have to try. Besides, maybe I'd learned something in the four years since I'd tried climbing the rope.

I watched as Dave scrambled up the rope. So did Matt and Jon for the Stanleys. Even Jill climbed to the top. First graders made it. I kept putting off my turn, letting more eager kids cut in front of me. Finally I couldn't put it off any longer. I stepped forward, grabbed the rope and lifted my feet to the knot. So far, so good. I reached up with my arms, tightened my grip and heaved. Nothing happened. I tried again and managed to pull myself an inch up with my arms. I began to turn red from effort and embarrassment. I struggled some more, but my long-legged body was too heavy for my arms.

I dropped off the rope, gulping back the sobs that threatened to explode. I moved behind the crowd, sniffing and dabbing at the corners of my eyes. Then someone behind me said, "You did your best. That's all that matters."

It was Jill. She'd seen me crying! I cleared my throat. "Thanks," I managed to mumble.

The rope climb was over and the teacher stood up to announce the score. "The Stanleys are ahead by five points and there's only one event left. The boys' soccer game is worth 20 points to the winning team. So whoever wins the soccer game will win this titchie field day. But right now we'll have a one-hour break for lunch. The soccer game will start at the field at 2 P.M."

Dave and I ran to get in line at the senior store. We each had a hamburger and a bottle of pop. As we sat down under a purple-flowered jacaranda tree to eat, Jill came up with the two new sixth grade girls. "Can we eat with you guys?" she asked.

Dave kind of froze up and couldn't answer so I said, "Sure."

"Have you met Rebekah and Rachel?" Jill asked. Dave and I shook our heads and I felt my cheeks turn red. Conversation with girls wasn't something we had practiced before and we weren't too good at it.

"They're new in school this year. Their parents work in Zaire translating the Bible. They've been home-schooled up until this year. So even though they're a year apart in age, they're both in sixth grade."

We asked how the hunting was in Zaire, but Rachel and Rebekah didn't know. Having exhausted our topics of conversation, Dave and I went back to eating and swigging our sodas.

We finished eating in silence. Then Dave and I stood up. "We've got to go play the soccer game," I said.

"If you win the game, the Livingstones will win titchie field day for the first time I can remember," Jill said.

"Yeah," I answered. Dave was already walking away.

"Well, I'll be cheering for you," Jill said, smiling at me.

"Thanks," I said, turning. My head felt like a balloon had

been inflated inside. I felt dizzy. I walked quickly to catch up with Dave.

"Why are you trembling, man?" Dave asked, noticing my excitement.

"I don't know."

"It's the girls. Come on, Dean. Focus. We have a soccer game to play and you're shaking because some girl talked to you."

"She smiled," I started.

"Soccer, Dean. Come on, man. We have to win."

Dave's words brought me back to reality. But I couldn't help but wonder if maybe Jill liked me a little.

Our Livingstone team captain called us over to get set for the game. He said he would play goalie. He put me at full-back and Dave at midfield. The whistle blew and Matt kicked off for the Stanleys. They worked the ball up quickly using short triangle passes. As usual, Jon ran in and started dribbling the ball. Matt slipped to the middle, just inside the goalkeeper's box. But as Jon crossed it to him, I stepped forward, cut off the pass and kicked it to Dave. Dave turned to pass it upfield but our center forward missed the trap and the Stanleys had the ball again.

We were pushed back against our goal most of the game. We just didn't have good enough players up front to keep the ball and score. Dave and I played our hearts out, but the Stanleys were better than we were. In the last five minutes, Matt hit the post after faking me out and firing on goal. I was able to get to the rebound and kick the ball down the hill. We only had one ball. So by kicking it down the hill we got to rest. Dave came over, panting. "Our forwards are never going to score. I'm going upfield and try to get a goal," he whispered to me. "Do your best to boot the ball up to me. It's our only chance."

Jon, who'd run down the hill to get the ball, got ready to take the throw in. I stood near Matt hoping to cut off the pass. Sure enough, Jon threw it straight to Matt. But Matt leaned back into me, protecting the ball. I wasn't too worried because Matt couldn't shoot with his back to the goal. Then Matt passed the ball back to his teammate Paul, who was right where Dave should have been. But Dave had gone upfield. Before any of our defenders could cover him, Paul trapped the ball, took two steps and slammed it at the goal. Our goalie saw the shot coming and dove to his left to block it. The shot was too hard for him to catch, but he punched it out. The ball rocketed straight toward my face. Before I could react, the ball smacked my forehead and flew straight into our own goal. I had scored for the Stanleys. I couldn't believe it!

I stood stunned. I didn't know what to say. I felt like crying, but how many times can a guy cry on one lousy field day? I bit my lower lip. Dave came back and patted my shoulder. "It's okay, Dean. Let's see if we can get the tying goal."

But my heart wasn't in it. A few minutes later the final whistle shrieked in my ear. I felt miserable. Our one chance to win titchie field day and I'd lost the soccer game by making a goal for the other team.

Matt and Jon both came over to shake my hand. "Good game, Dean," Matt said. "Sorry about the goal."

My tongue stuck to the back of my throat. I just nodded. I didn't have anything to say.

"Come on," Jon said, "I'll buy you a cola. We may be

Livingstones and Stanleys today, but the rest of the time we're the Rhinos and we're together."

Jill walked by. "Good try, Dean," she said. "It was a tough break but you did your best and that's all that really matters."

"Thanks," I replied. I felt a little better.

Jon ordered the colas. The senior reached elbow deep into the ice cold water in the big metal cooler and pulled out two dripping bottles. With a brisk motion he used the can opener to flick off the bottle lids with explosive pops. The caps flipped end over end and landed on the cracked cement. We each grabbed our bottle caps and peeled back the plastic foam lining to see if we'd won a prize in the latest bottlers' promotion. We each had soccer balls printed inside the caps, but they weren't red and black so we didn't win any prizes.

Just then we saw Dr. Freedman, Jon's dad, stride up to the store, his white coat flapping out behind him. He looked worried. "Did I miss your game, Jon?"

"Yeah, Dad," he said. "But that's okay. We won, but it was really close." Jon had learned to be understanding about his father's schedule as a doctor.

"I'm sorry," Dr. Freedman said. "I was on my way over here when they brought Kamau back to the hospital. Do you remember him? He was the boy you found near the pond."

"We remember him, Dad," Jon said. "I thought you said he got better."

"He did. We sent him home several weeks ago. Now his parents brought him back. He suddenly got very sick this morning."

"Is it the same sickness?" Matt asked.

"That's what's so strange," Dr. Freedman said. "The symptoms are completely different so it can't be. We're doing tests, but we can't seem to find the cause of this sickness either. Your praying helped save him the last time. I want you boys to pray again."

THE WITCH DOCTOR'S CURSE

"That's strange that Kamau is so sick again," Matt said.

"Makes it kind of hard to celebrate our victory." Then seeing my face he went on quickly, "I mean, here we are concerned about who wins a day's worth of games and Kamau may die."

I sighed. "Yeah, I guess you're right. I still feel bad for losing the field day with my own goal. But when you think of someone like Kamau being so sick it kind of puts things in perspective."

"Perspective? What kind of big word is that?" Matt demanded. "It sounds a lot like perspiration. That's a word I learned this week for a vocab test and it means sweat."

I knew Matt was trying to joke me out of feeling down. I

decided to let him. I stood up and punched him on the shoulder. "You know what I mean. I may be feeling sorry for myself for losing a soccer game and a field day, but at least I'm alive and healthy. Come on. Let's get out of here."

"Yeah, let's go for a hike," Jon suggested. "Did anyone check our genet cat trap today?"

No one had. We'd lost our enthusiasm for rising with the sun and the tropical birds to check the trap.

We hiked into the forest, field day almost forgotten and Kamau's sickness only a small dark cloud nagging in our minds.

Jon led the way followed by Matt. Dave and I were the tail-end-Charleys. I noticed Dave limping. "Are you all right?" I asked.

"I think so," he answered. "I hit someone's ankle pretty hard in the soccer game when I went for the ball. It feels like I have a bruise on my foot so I'm just taking it easy, that's all."

I slowed down to his pace. "It sure is peaceful down here under all these trees," Dave said, looking up.

I nodded. I could almost sense the presence of God in the forest. "Maybe that's why in the African traditional religions they felt that gods lived in certain trees."

"That's a weird thought, Dean," Dave said. "Where'd you come up with that?"

"My dad did some research on it for his magazine. I don't know why, but it just popped into my mind."

"Hurry up, you guys, or we'll never get there," Matt called.

We picked up the pace but I noticed Dave wincing, especially on downhill sections when he had to put a lot of pressure on his foot to keep from slipping.

As we came close to our trap site, Jon motioned to be

quiet. He crept up to the box, disturbing the ground as little as possible, then he came back shaking his head. "Nothing has even come near the trap."

"Maybe we should move it somewhere else," Matt suggested.

"Even more important than that, we need to put in fresh bait. The peanut butter has dried on the stick and it's so hard and grey that I think a genet cat would rather hurl than take a bite," Jon said with disgust. He wiped the stick against the tree, leaving a trail of peanut butter on its trunk.

"I didn't bring anything for bait," I said. No one else had either. We decided to come back another day with something different for bait. "Maybe a fish head," I suggested. "My dad often goes fishing at Lake Naivasha and catches bass."

"Sounds okay," Matt said, but I could tell he wasn't really interested. Building the trap had been a great idea, but since it hadn't caught anything he was ready to forget it. Matt liked things to happen right away. Waiting patiently for anything didn't agree with Matt.

"Let's go check our tree fort," Matt said, abruptly leading the way. "I feel like drinking some *chai*."

Dave looked a bit funny. And as we walked he dragged farther and farther behind. At the tree house, Jon scrambled up the tree and threw down the hanging ladder. Matt climbed up first. We could hear him rattling our big black kettle where we kept tea, sugar and powdered milk for our *chai* drinks in the forest. "Hey," he yelled down. "There's no sugar left. How can we drink *chai* without sugar? Dave, you're the treasurer. What happened?"

Dave looked up timidly. "I forgot," he said. "I noticed the last time that we had run out. And I know it's my job to take money from our dues and keep the clubhouse supplied. But with school and all, I just forgot. I'm sorry."

"I'm glad you're sorry, but that doesn't change our problem, Dave," Matt said. Sometimes Matt could get really annoyed. "I was looking forward to a nice mug full of sweet milky tea. And don't suggest that we drink *ndubia*, tea without sugar. Makes me shiver to think of drinking that stuff."

Dave climbed up the ladder, still favoring his sore foot. Picking up the small wooden box with the padlock he shook it and we could hear coins rattling inside. "We have money in our box," Dave suggested. "Why don't we take out enough to buy sugar, go to the *duka*—"

"But I'm in the mood to drink *chai* now," Matt cut in.

"You didn't let me finish," Dave said, calm as ever. "We can take out enough extra to buy a cup of *chai* and *mandazi* at the *chai* house while we're there buying the sugar. That way we can supply our tree house and have a good cup of *chai*. With *mandazi*, I might add, something you're not going to get here."

Matt was also quick to change moods. Now he smiled. "Sounds like a good plan. All in favor, vote yes." We all voted yes. Dave took the money from the box. We climbed down and set off for the *chai* house on the other side of Rugendo.

"*Muri ega?* Are you well?" the *chai* house owner greeted us in Kikuyu as we sat down on the wobbly bench behind a long table topped with wild-patterned formica.

Matt, the only Rhino who really understood Kikuyu, answered for all of us, "*Ii. Turi ega.* Yes, we are well." Then he ordered four mugs of *chai*, the sweet, milky Kenyan version of tea.

"Don't forget to buy some *mandazi*," Jon prompted.

"*Ongeza mandazi manne.* Add four *mandazi*," Dave said,

counting out the shillings for the *chai* and four *mandazi*, square, deep-fried pastries kind of like doughnuts but not nearly as sweet.

As we sucked noisily on our *chai* and dunked pieces of *mandazi* in the mugs to soften and sweeten them, two older Kikuyu men entered the *chai* house and sat down in the corner. Their foreheads wrinkled in concentration as they talked in hushed whispers.

I ignored them at first, savoring the *chai* and trying to forget my mistake in the soccer game. But the scene of heading the ball into our own goal kept repeating itself in my mind like my kid brother Craig rewinding and replaying his favorite parts of a cartoon on the video.

Then the Kikuyu men became agitated and one began speaking louder. The *chai* mugs on the table rocked back and forth and their *chai* spilled over the rims of the mugs. A small river of brown liquid headed toward our end of the table. It poured into a crack in the formica table top. *Chai* dripped off the table and soaked into the sawdust floor.

Matt's eyes widened like someone who's suddenly seen a leopard in a tree. "What's the matter, Matt?" I asked. "Scared the *chai* is going to drip all over your shorts and leave an embarrassing wet mark?"

Matt's eyes blazed as he signaled for me to be quiet. Then he leaned forward and said very quietly, "Something important has come up. Finish your *chai* and *mandazi* as quickly as possible. Then let's get out of here. But act natural."

I couldn't figure what had got into Matt. I looked at Dave with a puzzled frown. He shrugged.

I swirled the remaining *chai* in the bottom of my cup, watching bits of *mandazi* crumbs surfacing. Then I chugged it down and, in African fashion, gave a polite belch. We all stood up and thanked the *chai* house owner for the tea.

The two old men talked on, huddled together. They didn't notice our exit.

When we had gone a safe distance from the *chai* house Dave asked, "What's up, Matt? Why'd you make us leave so soon?"

"Didn't you hear those two men talking?" Matt asked.

We looked at each other. "Of course," Jon answered. "But I didn't understand a word of it. They were speaking in Kikuyu."

"I thought you guys could understand a little Kikuyu. Anyway, when they raised their voices and spilled the *chai*, one of the men said that Kamau's sickness had been caused by a curse. It seems that Ngugi's father called in a witch doctor who made the curse and that's why Kamau is sick again. The old men were arguing about whether to pass the news on to the church leaders. One said yes. The other said they should ignore it. He said if Kamau died, then it would be an even exchange and both families would forget the matter."

"I don't understand everything about this, but it gives me the creeps," Jon said, shivering a little. "Ngugi's father scared me that day in the hospital when he threatened to get his revenge on Kamau's family. We'd better go tell my dad."

The four of us hustled over to Jon's house. We ran up the driveway, lined by yellow and green century cactus plants. Their long leaves lolled onto the ground like tongues from a tired dog. We saw Jon's dad picking lemons from his tree.

"Dad, Dad," Jon burst out. "We just found out why Kamau's sick. Ngugi's father got a witch doctor to put a curse on him!"

chapter six

DEMONIC ATTACK

Dr. Freedman stepped out from under his lemon tree and looked at us with a puzzled frown. "What did you say?" he asked.

"We said Kamau's sickness is caused by a witch doctor's curse. Ngugi's father went to the witch doctor to get revenge on Kamau's family," Jon said urgently. "Come on, Dad, you've got to do something."

"Hold on, Jon," his dad said, chuckling. "Now, I know Kamau is very sick, but I doubt very much if a witch doctor has anything to do with it. Witch doctors just play on old tribal fears and superstitions. They use gimmicks like throwing bones. I watched one at work when we first arrived here in Africa. He looked impressive. The child he was examining had small oozing sores all over his body. The witch doctor said he had discerned the cause of the disease. No one in the family had given an offering to their deceased grandfather. He told the family they had to sacrifice a goat and plead with the dead grandfather to forgive them for not remembering him. When the ancestor was happy, he might ask God to heal their child. The family brought the goat. The witch doctor did the sacrifice and said it was successful. Then he kept a large share of the goat meat and charged the family two chickens for his services."

"Well, what happened?" Jon asked.

"The child got better. But I had looked at the child closely. All he had was chicken pox. He'd have gotten better even without the sacrifice. So the witch doctor made out pretty well on that one. I think witch doctors are just fooling people. But, tell me, why do you boys think Kamau's sickness is caused by a witch doctor's curse? The African people are not very open about sharing that kind of stuff, especially not with missionaries or their kids."

"I overheard two older men talking about it in the *chai* house," Matt said. "They were arguing over whether to tell the church leaders or not. They sounded serious."

"Well, maybe I'll have Pastor Waweru check into it. Like I said, I don't really believe witch doctors have any power. Besides, Kamau and his family are faithful Christians. I don't think much will come of this, but we'll see what Pastor Waweru finds out."

The next day I went to church with my parents. The service always seemed to last so long. They translated the sermon from Kikuyu to English. When the translator finished and the preacher went on in Kikuyu, I would stop listening. The trouble was, I never managed to listen again when the translator picked up. When I tuned in again, I'd get confused. This Sunday morning my mind kept going over the soccer game. I replayed it a hundred times in my mind. But in my mind, I didn't knock the ball into our own goal. Instead, I made a magnificent chest trap, turned and passed the ball up field to where Dave waited. The pass sliced perfectly between the defenders. Dave pounded in the winning goal, just nicking the corner post.

Suddenly everyone was standing up. It was time for the last hymn. I hadn't learned anything from the sermon, but my daydreaming had made the time pass quickly. I looked over to where Matt and Jon sat. I sighed as I realized my daydreaming hadn't changed the score from the day before. We'd still lost the game.

After church we Rhinos walked home together. We stopped off in the garden at Jon's house to pick some black raspberries. As we snaked our hands in between the thorny branches to get the berries, we heard two men talking. Turning, I saw Dr. Freedman walking up the road with Pastor Waweru.

Matt signaled to get down. We crouched beside the berry bush and listened.

"This is a very serious matter, Dr. Freedman," Pastor Waweru said. "I went to see Ngugi's father. At first he denied everything. Then I asked some of the neighbors and they confirmed that a well-known *mganga*, or witch doctor, had visited Ngugi's father. So I went back to him. This time he admitted he had called in the witch doctor. But he said it was none of our business. If Kamau died it would prove Kamau's family had been to blame for Ngugi's death."

Dr. Freedman still looked skeptical. "I still don't think

the witch doctor has the power of life and death over Kamau."

"He doesn't," agreed Pastor Waweru, "but he is in touch with spiritual forces that have the power to attack and bring sickness and even death. Even the Bible confirms this, Dr. Freedman. Haven't you read Luke 13? There was a woman in the synagogue who had been crippled by a spirit. When Jesus healed her on the Sabbath he said Satan had held the woman in bondage for eighteen years. And of course Job and his family were attacked by Satan. Job's children were killed."

"But that was years ago," the doctor began. "Surely, in this day and age—"

Pastor Waweru held his arms open wide as he interrupted, "In this day and age Satan is still alive and well. He has no more power than God allows him as we can see from the story of Job. But we give Satan and his demons all sorts of room to attack when we refuse to believe he even exists."

"Of course I believe Satan exists," Dr. Freedman said. "But—"

"You say it with your mouth," Pastor Waweru cut in, "but to really believe in something you have to believe it in your head and your heart. You have to act on your belief. My people say, 'Kusema na kufanya ni mambo tofaut.' To speak and to do are different matters." He turned to walk away.

"Wait," Dr. Freedman called, and he hustled after the pastor. He caught Pastor Waweru by the shoulder. They talked, but we couldn't hear anything now that they had moved down the road. They soon returned to Jon's house. The two men climbed into the Freedmans' Land Rover. The big diesel engine belched out a cloud of dark black smoke as it started up, then bounced down the driveway.

We all looked at each other. "I wonder where they're going?" I asked.

"Probably to talk with Ngugi's father or something," Jon said. "Well, I haven't had lunch yet and these berries are sweet but they're not filling me up." He ran down to his house.

"Let's meet here at two and ride bikes," Matt called.

"All right," Jon said before he slammed the door.

"See you guys this afternoon," I said.

After a wonderful Sunday dinner of roast wart hog from my dad's recent hunting trip and mashed potatoes from our garden plus a rhubarb pie with homemade ice cream, I felt so full I could hardly sit.

I asked to be excused and flopped down on the couch. "Aah, that feels better," I said as I stretched out.

"Actually," my mom said, "there's an even better position after you've eaten too much. Standing up over the sink and washing the dishes."

"Washing dishes! Mom, can't they soak until tomorrow?"

She smiled patiently. But her answer was firm. "No."

Craig started clearing the dirty dishes. "Why do I always have to clear?" he whined.

"You could always swap with me," I said. "Washing is great fun. You can make bubbles in the water and slop water onto the floor and make everyone slip."

Craig brightened. "Can I?"

"No," my mom said. "Craig is not old enough to wash yet. Now get on with your work, Dean."

My dad said, "I'll dry the dishes. I'm supposed to be at an elders meeting at church, but it won't start for another half hour."

As we worked side by side, I asked my dad if he knew about Kamau.

"I heard he was sick again and they couldn't figure out what was wrong."

I debated whether to tell him about what we'd overheard in the *chai* house. Then I decided to go for it. I knew my dad had done some research on African traditional religions for his magazine. So I said, "We Rhinos heard Kamau's sickness was caused by a witch doctor's curse."

My dad turned immediately. "Where'd you hear this?"

"Matt overheard two old men talking at the *chai* house yesterday."

"Yesterday! Why didn't you tell me right away?"

"We did tell Jon's dad, but he didn't think it was important. So we didn't tell anyone else."

"Dr. Freedman didn't do anything about it?" my dad asked.

"Well, he said he would talk to Pastor Waweru and then today we heard them talking about it near Jon's house. Pastor said he'd found out there really had been a witch doctor involved. But Dr. Freedman still didn't think it had much to do with Kamau's sickness. They argued a bit and then drove off in the Freedmans' Land Rover."

"I've got to talk to him right away. Let's go," my dad said, dropping his dish towel.

"Honey, what about the dishes?" my mom called after us.

"We'll take care of them later. There's an emergency," my dad answered.

At Jon's house we found Mrs. Freedman cleaning up after their meal. I noticed Jon didn't have to help. She had left one clean plate on the table. "Where'd your husband go?" my dad asked.

"He and Pastor Waweru went to visit some family about a mile away. I'm not sure where." She didn't look very happy. "He hardly ever gets to sit down for a meal with us anymore," she sighed. "But he said he'd be back soon so I'm keeping his food hot."

Just then Dr. Freedman drove up. He walked in the door, shaking off the dust. He looked scared, just like Matt did the time he'd tripped on the edge of a steep ravine only inches away from a twenty-foot drop.

My dad walked over to him. "Are you all right?"

Dr. Freedman nodded. "Yeah, I think so." He sat down shakily. Jon's mom looked concerned as she served her husband's meal.

"What's wrong, Dad?" Jon asked.

"I've just come face-to-face with deep, bitter anger," he said slowly, carefully.

"What do you mean?" my dad asked.

Taking a deep breath, Dr. Freedman said, "Let me explain." He told my dad how we Rhinos had overheard the men talking about the witch doctor. "At first I didn't believe it was anything serious. But today Pastor Waweru opened my eyes. Kamau could be suffering from some sort of demonic attack. So we went to see Ngugi's father. He told us Kamau would die because he had asked a witch doctor to unleash powerful spiritual forces against him. I said Kamau's family had nothing to do with Ngugi's death."

He stopped to take a few bites of his supper.

"What happened next?" my dad asked.

Dr. Freedman shook his head. "I've never seen anyone so angry. His eyes rolled, his body literally shook. He seemed to be consumed, controlled by his anger. I've never seen anything like it. It frightened me. He told me I was abusing him. Not only would Kamau die, but he would call in the witch doctor this very afternoon and bring another curse on someone else here at Rugendo. Then he marched away.

"Pastor Waweru said prayer was the only answer. So I dropped him off at the church elders' meeting and they said they would be praying. But I don't know. How can a witch doctor's curse bring on physical sickness? Sickness and disease are caused by germs, not by African spirits."

My dad put his arm on Dr. Freedman's shoulder. "There's more to this than you understand. Actually, Pastor Waweru had the right answer. We have to pray. I'm going over to meet with the church elders and we'll see how to handle this."

"Thanks," Dr. Freedman said, looking drained.

"It's scary to meet up with the powers of darkness like this," my dad said. "But don't worry. In the name of Jesus we have the power and the victory."

After my dad left, I asked Jon to get his bike so we could ride.

"I don't know," said Jon. "I just started getting a really bad headache."

chapter seven

A
FRIGHTENING
SICKNESS

"Maybe you'd better rest, Jon," his dad said without looking up from his plate of food.

"Yeah, I'll see you later, Jon," I said. "I hope you feel better." Then I slipped out of the house.

I met Matt and Dave and we rode bikes for a while. But it wasn't the same without Jon. He usually rode like crazy, dodging between trees and making jumps over—and into—ditches. Matt, a wild rider himself, could always count on Jon to keep our rides exciting. But Dave and I weren't into bike accidents so we didn't keep up like Matt wanted.

"I'm bored," Matt announced. "Let's do something different."

"Like what?" I asked, not sure what to expect.

Matt thought for a while. Then he jumped up. "I've got it. We can have a faith ride. You know, like the faith walk we had at youth group last Sunday night. It's where you have to close your eyes and trust your partner to guide you by voice commands. Only we can do it riding our bikes. Dave, you can go first. Dean, you be second, and I'll go last."

I looked at Dave. He didn't look very excited about the idea. But neither of us wanted to tell Matt no.

"Let's go to that circle next to the mission guest house," Matt said. "That will make it challenging and exciting at the same time. It will be hard to ride a bike around the traffic circle with your eyes closed and if you go off the road, you guys might ride off the bank or into the drainage ditch on the other side. Man, what a great idea!"

We followed Matt like chickens on the way to the chopping stump. At the circle he got off his bike. "Okay, Dave, close your eyes and start riding. We'll tell you when and where to turn."

Dave's face turned the color of the paste my dad uses at his office for laying out pages of his magazine. But he pushed off and wobbled around the circle following our shouted directions, "Left! Left! No, now turn right! Watch out for the ditch! Left, we said!"

After Dave rode around the circle without crashing, Matt motioned to me. I got on my bike and started. I felt terrified. I could hear them shouting instructions, but in my mind I was sure I was headed for the bank or the ditch. I peeked a little to see where I was. To my amazement I was actually on the road.

I closed my eyes again and forced myself to follow Matt's and Dave's directions. But I kept peeking, just to be sure.

When I finished, Matt said with disgust, "You guys went around like a couple of pansies. Let me show you how to really ride in faith." He hopped on his bike and pedaled like crazy. Dave and I managed to say left once. But Matt was going so hard and fast toward the bank that we froze. Matt shouted, "Which way do I turn? Come on, which way?"

He looked so funny steaming toward the bank with his eyes shut tight that Dave and I started to giggle and we couldn't tell him anything. Then Matt flew off the edge of the road and tumbled down the bank.

We ran over to where Matt was rubbing his head and pulling himself out from under his bent bike. "Why didn't you tell me to turn? You guys are a bunch of *nugus* [baboons]."

Dave got to him first. "Ouch," Matt said, gently touching a lump on his forehead. "That hurts."

Dave helped him stand up and they examined his cuts and scratches. "Now we're all wounded," Dave said. "I've got a sore foot and you've got bumps and bruises. Jon has a headache."

"What about me?" I asked.

"You have a sore heart after yesterday's game," Matt said. Then he saw my face. "Hey, I'm sorry," he apologized.

"I guess we all know what it means to hurt," I said.

I gripped Matt's front wheel between my knees and straightened out the handlebars. Matt bent over and ripped out the spoke that had come loose. "I'm sure it will ride just as well without one spoke," he said. We rode by Jon's house to see how he was feeling. His mom answered the door.

"How's Jon?" Matt asked.

"I'm afraid he has a high fever to go along with his headache," she answered. "Thanks for coming by. I'll tell him you were here. What happened to you, Matt?" Jon's mom pointed to the bump on Matt's head.

"Just a slight bike wreck," Matt said, smiling. He always liked the attention he got from an injury. "I'll be fine."

"I hope Jon gets better," Dave said.

The next morning, Jon was not in school. At lunch my parents told me that Jon was in the hospital with a dangerously high fever. "They're doing the blood test for malaria," Mom said. "But I doubt it will show anything. The Freedmans haven't been away from Rugendo in two months and this place at 8,000 feet is too high for mosquitoes."

That night I heard that even though the test for malaria had been negative they were treating Jon for malaria anyway. During our family devotions I asked if we could pray for both Jon and Kamau. My dad agreed.

"Dear Lord," I prayed, "please help Jon and Kamau to get better. We don't know what kind of sickness they have. But I know you are God. Help them. In Jesus' name, Amen."

Craig's five-year-old prayer was even shorter. "Dear Jesus, make Jon and Kamau get better. Amen."

Mom and Dad both prayed like typical grown-ups and went on for a long time. I noticed they prayed something I hadn't heard them pray before. They prayed about putting on God's armor. They prayed for God's protection over Jon and Kamau in the name of Jesus and by the power of his blood. They also asked God to bind Satan and his forces.

After our prayers I asked them why they had prayed differently. My dad explained, "We really believe that both

Kamau's and Jon's sickness are caused by evil spirits so we prayed spiritual warfare type of prayers."

"What's spiritual warfare?" I asked.

"When Paul wrote to the Christians at Ephesus, he told them that we Christians are in a battle. It's a spiritual battle." He reached over for his well-worn Bible and flipped quickly toward the end. As I balanced on my stomach on the back of the couch and looked over his shoulder, I saw verses that had been heavily underlined with a red marker. He looked up. "The Bible in Ephesians chapter 6 talks about putting on God's spiritual armor so we can stand against Satan. So I was just praying like a soldier getting ready for the battle."

I felt scared. "You don't think Jon is going to die, do you?"

Dad's face looked grim. "I don't know," he said. "But I know we've got a battle on our hands. Jon got sick right after the witch doctor's threat to put a curse on someone else besides Kamau. God tells us that the victory is ours, but we must be alert and pray."

"But why Jon?" I asked.

Dad looked at me. "I'm not sure. I do know Satan often attacks those who are the weakest. That's why one of the pieces of armor listed here is the breastplate of righteousness. None of us is righteous. But when we believe in Jesus, God forgives us and cleanses us. We are forgiven. That's our righteousness. If we take a look at our lives every day we can make sure our armor is on so Satan can't attack."

This last sermon kind of went beyond me. I had to let Dad help me get it straight when I wrote this story up for our Rugendo Rhino records. But it made me feel grown up to have my dad talk to me like that. And I understood how dangerous Jon's sickness was.

The next day we heard that Jon and Kamau were both worse. The fevers soared. Malaria medicine hadn't done anything. They couldn't find any physical cause for the illnesses and so far their bodies weren't responding to any treatment. At lunch time my dad told me the church elders had called an all-station prayer meeting for that evening to deal with the spiritual attack on Rugendo.

"Can I come?" I asked.

Mom was shaking her head, but Dad paused and then said, "Yes. We have the right to claim protection over you. Just make sure all your sins are confessed up to date."

I spent most of the afternoon thinking through different things I'd done wrong, confessing them to God and asking for his forgiveness. I also asked Craig to forgive me for teasing and bullying him. "And I'm especially sorry for taking the nylon stockings out of the stuffed toy monkey that Mom made for you and giving them to our puppies," I said.

At the prayer meeting I sat with my parents. Most of the missionaries came in with worried looks on their faces. There were a few whispered greetings. One of the men started the meeting by leading hymns while we waited for others to arrive. An older lady played the battered upright piano in the front of the meeting hall. After about ten minutes Pastor Waweru arrived with a group of Kenyans. Most of them were church elders.

The church pastor was there along with the headmaster of the Kenyan high school. I also noticed Kamau's parents. Most of the Kenyans looked uncomfortable. The station meeting hall was usually used for missionary meetings. But the men had decided the big church would be too large for the prayer meeting. My dad got up and welcomed the group of Kenyans, ushering them to seats near the front.

Dad stood in front of the group. "As you know," he said, "we've called this meeting to pray for young Kamau and Jon Freedman. They're both very sick with no apparent cause except that we hear a witch doctor has put a curse on them at Ngugi's father's request. Most of you will remember that Ngugi is the boy who died earlier this month. We feel the sicknesses are linked to some sort of spiritual attack, and as Christians we must get on our knees before God and pray to win this battle. I've asked Pastor Waweru to tell us about spiritual warfare. Some of us from the West might be less likely to believe in the power of spiritual forces."

"That's where I have a question," said one of the missionaries, a tomato-faced school teacher. "I believe in Satan and his power. But if Jon and Kamau are both believers and their parents are believers, how can Satan touch them? I agree we need to pray. But I don't feel this is a spiritual attack."

"Fair enough," my father answered. "That's why I've asked Pastor Waweru to speak to us first. We need to be united in prayer."

My dad stepped aside and Pastor Waweru stood up. He started with a short prayer of blessing before starting. "Satan has power," he said, with a smile, "but Jesus Christ has much more power! That's the good news tonight. Let me tell you how demonic forces can attack believers."

Just then the station intercom phone rang. The lady who answered it waved Dr. Freedman over. I watched him talk on the phone at the back of the room. I could see his face wrinkle into a frown as he listened. He almost dropped the phone then said with a choking voice, "Jon and Kamau are both having trouble breathing. Please keep praying. I have to go see what I can do. But it looks like they're near the end." Tears glistened in his eyes as he ran out the door.

chapter eight

SPIRITUAL WARFARE PRAYING

Everyone listened intently as Pastor Waweru led the prayer meeting. "We need to pray, but we must be prepared first. Satan's forces, demons, do have power. But Jesus is in control over them, too.

"Paul wrote in Ephesians that we have the right to do battle with Satan in the name of Jesus. We have the authority.

"You see, in the past we Africans lived in fear of spiritual forces. Our fears were well-founded. The witch doctors had contact with spirits, but they had no real power. Our old way of life consisted of making sacrifices to the spirits, who we thought were departed ancestors. We poured out beer and left out food for them. We thought the spirits of our ancestors would be pleased. They would speak to God for us and give us a peaceful life. Whenever anything bad happened, we immediately assumed we had offended some spirit." Pastor Waweru paced back and forth for a few moments before continuing.

"My father was a young boy when the first missionaries came. Those first missionaries taught that if we believed in Jesus we had power against spiritual attacks. That's why so many people came to Christ. We weren't running to a Western religion. We were running for safety.

"Even though people felt the spirits were our dead forefathers, they were really demons sent from Satan to torment us."

The same school teacher raised his hand. "But how can we be sure this is a spiritual attack? I've always understood that believers can't be hurt by Satan."

Pastor Waweru nodded and answered, "Sometimes it is hard to know when a sickness is caused by spiritual forces or some physical illness." He smiled. "But in this case we know spiritual forces have brought the sicknesses. And Christians can be vulnerable to satanic attack. Ephesians 4:27 says that if we leave anger in our hearts overnight we give the devil a place where he can get a grip on us."

Suddenly I was glad I'd asked Craig to forgive me for teasing him.

My dad cut in, "We also have to remember that Job, a God-fearing man, was attacked by Satan to test his faith. The first step in spiritual warfare praying is for all of us to confess our sins. Then we can go on and claim the victory." He looked at Pastor Waweru. "I think we should go to prayer now."

Pastor Waweru nodded and led the group in a time of

confession. Then he gave a chance for silent prayer. He told each person to pray asking God to examine his or her own heart. I had a hard time keeping my eyes closed and I noticed a number of people crying. After that Pastor said if anyone had to make anything right with anyone else, this was the time to do it. I peeked and could see a number of the people hugging each other and whispering.

My dad then explained why spiritual armor was important and led a prayer so the people could put on their armor and be protected. As Dad spoke, I imagined myself pulling on a shiny silver breastplate of righteousness. In my mind I wore a decorated helmet of salvation and raised my shield of faith in triumph.

"Now we need to praise the Lord," my dad said. "In 2 Chronicles 22, when King Jehoshaphat went out to battle against Moab and Ammon, he put the singers in front of the soldiers. Let's praise the Lord in song and watch his answer." We spent some time singing praise songs, but I'll admit I liked being a soldier more than singing.

After we sang, everyone prayed. Kenyans and missionaries alike called on God to save Kamau and Jon. Some said prayers binding Satan and his demons. Others confessed sins or reminded God of his promises. I just knew God would answer.

After almost two hours of praying, Dr. Freedman walked in. Instantly, the prayers hushed. Everyone turned and the doctor struggled to speak. Finally he managed, "I think we're going to lose them. Nothing we've done makes any difference." Kamau's parents came over to him along with Mrs. Freedman, who burst into tears. "We're going to the hospital to be with our boys." The grieving parents held onto each other as they walked out of the meeting hall. I felt as if I'd just had all the air knocked out of me.

No one spoke for what seemed like hours. "Looks like we've failed," the school teacher with the red face said, finally. All over the room people hung their heads. A lady sitting in back of me began to cry softly.

Then my dad stood up. "The battle is not over yet. We can't retreat. I'm sure we are making progress and we need to pray on to victory. Remember the story about the man who brought his son to Jesus to be delivered from a spirit? When Jesus asked the father if he believed he could cast the spirit out, the father answered, 'I do believe; help me overcome my unbelief.' Let's close this meeting by asking God to help us win the fight. Then anyone who feels up to it can go down to the hospital and pray at the bedside of the two boys. Everyone else can go on home. But keep praying."

After the final prayer, the meeting broke up and I went home with my mom. I wanted to keep on praying in my room but as soon as I hit the bed I fell asleep.

When I woke up in the morning and stumbled down the stairs the heavy aroma of Kenyan coffee filled the kitchen. I found Mom and Dad sitting at the dining room table eating toast and drinking coffee. Dad had gray circles under his eyes and his beard stubble made him look a lot older. But he was smiling.

"Good news!" he said. "Kamau and Jon are getting better! God answered our prayers!"

"What happened?" I asked, sitting down. Mom popped two slices of bread into the toaster.

"We were up for hours last night. We made a circle around Jon's and Kamau's beds. We felt like we'd moved into the very presence of God. Those Kenyan pastors really know how to pray. Suddenly it seemed like a spirit of peace fell on the room like a blanket. We knew God was right there. Then we were silent, and suddenly both Kamau and Jon started to breathe more easily. Dr. Freedman was the most surprised. I think he'd given up hope. He touched the boys and said the fever had broken on both of them. We thanked God and praised him for winning the victory just as he promised."

"Oh, no!" my mom said, jumping up. "The toast!" Smoke curled out of the toaster. The automatic popper-upper had burned out the year before. She grabbed the two charred slices and opened up the window to fling them outside.

"God really can answer prayer," I said. "I'm sure glad they're going to be all right."

Someone pounded on our door. I went to open it and found Matt and Dave. "Hey, did you hear Jon and Kamau are better?" I began.

"Yeah, our dads both went and prayed at the hospital last night," Matt said. "Aren't you ready for school yet?"

"Give me five minutes. Come on in and wait. Mom! I'll just have bread. Don't bother to try to toast it." I ran upstairs to get dressed.

I grabbed the peanut butter and jam sandwich from my mom as I walked out the door.

"Do you remember what day today is?" Matt asked.

I frowned. "I guess I forgot. The day Jon and Kamau got better?"

"Yes," said Dave, "but it's also the day we get our kits for Pinewood Derby. Boy, do I have the greatest plan worked out. I'm going to make a Toyota Celica Safari Rally car."

"That's right!" I said. "Pinewood Derby! I forgot

completely after Jon got sick. I have no idea what kind of car I'll make."

"Me either," said Matt. "But I know mine will be fast." Matt never spent too much time with the finer parts of sanding and painting. His car always looked like a block of wood. He concentrated on the wheels. And his cars were always fast.

"We'd better remember to pick up a kit for Jon," I said. "I'm sure he can get started on it as he gets better."

"What a day," Dave said. "Jon's better. Kamau's better. And it's the start of the Pinewood Derby. All right!"

chapter nine

PINEWOOD DERBY

Loud clapping prevented the woodshop teacher from giving his chapel announcement. Those of us who had been at school for awhile knew he'd be telling us when and where to pick up our Pinewood Derby kits. We were so excited we just started clapping and cheering. The teacher smiled, one hand waving to quiet us down. When our cheering stopped, he held up a great-looking Model-T Ford he had made last year. Then he explained what the Derby was all about.

The Pinewood Derby is a car race. But first we had to build the cars. Everyone who wanted to enter would get a kit that contained a rectangular block of wood, two axles, four plastic wheels and four nails to hold the wheels on the axles. Each person had to design his or her own car and then carve it. The teacher told us we could get help from teachers in the woodshop during certain hours after school. They could help make the big cuts with electric saws if we marked our blocks where we wanted the cuts made. Of course they would offer advice as well. Then it was up to us to sand the blocks, making them as smooth as possible before painting.

Everyone would have to have their cars completed in about three weeks. On Pinewood Derby weekend the cars would be displayed and judges would give prizes for things like creativity and best workmanship. There would be awards for each age group. Then, on Saturday, we would have the race. The woodshop teacher had built a race track especially for the cars. When all the pieces of the race track were set up, the track filled one end of the school auditorium. The track started as high as the ceiling. The teachers stood on ladders to put the cars in the starting area. Thin strips of wood divided the lanes and five cars could race at once. The track dropped off very steeply so the cars could gain speed; then they would go over a gentle hump before the final straightaway. On race day there would be heats and then the championships.

Even though I'd heard the announcement every year it still excited me and made me want to get out there and win. I'd never won any awards. Not for workmanship, that's for sure. I had a hard time doing things neatly. Dave, on the other hand, had two trophies for workmanship. His cars always looked *safi*, the Swahili word for clean, and to us kids it meant anything really cool. I'd never won any speed awards either. I remembered the year before when my car had run so poorly it hadn't made it to the end of the track. I'd blown on the wheels and oiled the nails that held the axles. Nothing had helped. But maybe this year I'd get lucky.

After school Matt, Dave, and I went to the woodshop to pick up our kits. "Can we have a kit for Jon, too?" Matt asked.

"Sure," the teacher answered. "I heard he's getting better. But Jon won't be back in school yet, will he?"

"I don't think so," Matt said. "But if he has the kit he can look at it and plan how he's going to make his car when he comes back."

We stopped by Jon's house to see if we could get permission to visit him in the hospital. To our surprise, his mom said he was already at home, resting in bed. We all trooped into Jon's bedroom. His head was propped up on a pile of pillows.

"You feeling better?" Matt asked.

"Yeah," Jon said, and then yawned. "Just tired. I'm more tired than the day we tried to run all the way up Mt. Longonot. But, yeah, I'm feeling better. Thanks."

"For what?" Matt asked.

"For praying. My dad said that if people hadn't prayed I'd have probably died. And Kamau, too. That's scary."

"But God did answer," I said. "And we're all thankful for that."

"Yeah, we're glad you're okay," Dave said.

"We brought you a present," Matt said, pulling out the plastic bag with the Pinewood Derby kit.

"Pinewood Derby!" Jon said, his eyes brightening. "All right! I'll have to get well right away so I can build my car. I'm going to win the race this year."

"Me, too," said Matt. "My car will be pure speed."

"What design are you going to make?" Dave asked us.

"I'm not sure," Matt said. "But it will be fast."

"I want mine to be shaped like a Porsche 911," Jon said.

"Mine's going to look like a Toyota Celica," Dave said. "I have a picture of Bjorkman from the last Safari Rally and I'm going to make mine look like that. What about you, Dean?"

"Well, I was thinking of making mine look like a banana. I thought it might win a prize for creativity and still go kind of fast."

The other guys eyed me as if I was a vervet monkey that had just jumped down out of a tree. I could tell they didn't think much of my idea.

Dave responded first. "Well, Dean, that sounds...interesting. Yes, very interesting." Then all three began chattering about what they were going to do with their cars. I took out my block of wood and tapped it absently in my palm. I'd have to come up with some great idea!

I didn't have the patience for detail work like Dave so I had little chance of winning for workmanship. I'd love to win the racing part. My dad had promised to help me with my wheels this year. He said the wheels had more to do with speed than design. I still thought a banana was a pretty good idea, but if the other kids were going to laugh about it, then I'd have to think of something else.

After about half an hour Jon's mom came in and herded us out. "Jon needs to rest," she said. We could tell she was happy, though—happy that Jon was going to be all right.

We had hot dogs for supper. My little brother Craig took a big bite out of the middle of his and hit a chunk of cartilage. Pieces like that often surfaced in the hot dogs sold in Kenya. Craig didn't like it at all. He gagged and spit it out onto his plate while jumping back from the table. "What is that?" he demanded. Dad explained what hot dogs were made from and that sometimes parts like cartilage didn't get cut up well.

"I'm not eating that! Yuk!" Craig said and ran to his room. As I looked at his hot dog laying in the bun with a large bite out of it, something clicked in my mind.

"Yes!" I said out loud.

"Yes, what?" Mom asked.

"Craig's hot dog gives me a great idea for my Pinewood Derby car. I think I'm going to make mine look like a bun with a hot dog in it and one large bite taken out. I could paint the hot dog orange-red and then paint yellow mustard and red ketchup on it."

"Sounds different," Dad said.

"It has to be different to win the creativity prize," I said. "Remember the one last year that looked like a giant pencil? And the one that looked like the space shuttle?"

My parents nodded. "And the shape should run fairly fast if we get your wheels fixed on straight," Dad said. "Remember I told you I'd help you with that this year?"

"Yeah, I remember," I said. "How could I forget. Last year my front wheels finished the first heat before my car did."

Craig poked his head around the corner. "Do I have to eat my hot dog?" he asked.

Mom had pity. "No, Craig. Come, I'll fix you a bowl of cereal."

"Can I have his hot dog?" I asked.

Mom raised her eyebrows. "You want to eat it?"

"No," I said. "I want to use it as my model for making my car."

She looked at me as I took a crinkled piece of aluminum foil from the cupboard and wrapped up the hot dog and bun.

When Craig saw that I wanted his supper, he said, "I want to eat my hot dog now."

"With that gross chunk of rubbery stuff in it?" I teased.

"Dean!" my mother said sharply.

But my words had already had their desired effect. Craig's face paled. "Maybe I don't really want it," he said, turning away.

Later in my room I took out my block of wood. Using Craig's unfinished dinner as my model, I drew some pencil lines along both sides of the block where I wanted the woodshop teacher to cut the wood with the band saw. Midway down the length of the block I drew in a jagged half-moon section that would look like a bite mark.

I squinted at the block of wood, rotating it to see it from different angles. I got out my eraser and rubbed out one of the lines, carefully drawing the line a bit higher. Satisfied, I put the block in the plastic bag to take to woodshop the next day. I couldn't wait to start shaping and sanding my car.

Then I got into bed to read my Bible. After reading chapter 3 of John, I saw the plastic bag on my desk. I began to wonder if the other Rhinos would laugh at me for making a hot dog car. I decided not to take any chances. I got up and took the real hot dog out of the foil and wrapped the foil around the block of wood. Then, feeling a bit hungry, I ate Craig's hot dog.

The next day after school we all ran to the woodshop. I stood in line with Matt and Dave. They showed me the lines they'd drawn on their blocks and described how great their cars would look. I glanced down at my block in its aluminum foil wrapper. How would I get it cut without the other guys seeing my design? I remembered Jon. "I wonder if

Jon drew his design yet? Maybe I should run down to his house and bring up his block to be cut."

"Yeah, we should have thought of that earlier," Matt said. I could tell he didn't want to lose his place in line. Neither did Dave. They wanted to get on with the finish work of carving and sanding.

"You guys go ahead," I said. "I'm in no hurry to get my block cut. I'll run on down and get Jon's kit and then get his and mine cut together. The woodshop is open until five-thirty."

I found Jon resting on the couch. "My dad says I can go back to school tomorrow," he said. "I feel like I'm ready now, but he says I still need to rest. I hate resting. Look. The sun's shining and it's beautiful outside."

I smiled. "I'm really glad you're feeling better. I came to see if you had your design drawn on your car. I could take it and get it cut on the band saw so you could work on it. It might give you something to do the rest of today."

"Sounds good," said Jon, jumping off the couch and running into his bedroom. He brought out his block of wood. The rough pencil marks along the side would give his car an arrow-shaped front end and a squared-off back. "It's not exactly like a Porsche 911," Jon said, "but it's close enough. I think it will be really fast. Look at that front end. It'll slice through the air."

I took both our blocks back up to the woodshop. Matt and Dave were nowhere to be seen. They must have had their wood cut and gone home to continue working.

The line was short so I wouldn't have to wait long. I didn't notice who was in front of me until Jill turned around.

"Hi, Dean," she said with a big smile. "What's your car going to look like this year?"

I felt my face turning hot and red.

THE HOT DOG CAR

"Here's what I'm planning," Jill said, taking out her block of wood. "I thought I'd make a bathtub at first, but then my dad told me I'd have to chisel out the inside of the tub. That sounded like a lot of work. So I decided to do this."

She held the wood near my face. I looked at it closely and smiled. "It looks great! What's it supposed to be?"

"You can't tell?" she asked, a frown wrinkling her usually pretty face.

"Well, it's hard to tell what anything is going to look like just from the pencil marks. Why don't you describe it to me?"

She brightened. "It's going to be a Maasai milk gourd. You know, the kind that is shaped like a sausage. I'll have it cut in that shape and then paint it brown. My mother even said I could borrow the beautiful beaded stopper off a real Maasai gourd they bought as a souvenir. I'll put that over the nose of the car. And my dad said he'd help me tack a leather strap on the top."

"Sounds like a great idea," I said. "The only thing left is for you to make it smell smoky just like the inside of a real milk gourd."

She laughed and that made me feel good.

"And what's your car going to look like this year?" Jill asked. "It must be top secret. It's all wrapped in aluminum foil."

I made sure Matt and Dave weren't around. Then I whispered. "It's going to look like a hot dog."

"A hot rod? What kind of hot rod?" She looked a little puzzled.

"No, not a hot *rod*," I explained. "A hot *dog*."

I said this last part a bit too loudly. Several people turned and looked at us. I tried to ignore them. I took out my pinewood block and showed it to Jill.

"I think that will look really *safi*," she said.

It was Jill's turn to have her wood cut. The teacher placed it on the band saw and quickly made the cuts. I waved good-bye as she left the woodshop. Then I handed both my block and Jon's to the woodshop teacher. I didn't bother to tell him whose was whose in case he thought the hot dog idea was weird. But with the band saw humming, he simply sliced off the extra wood. I would have to do a lot of chiseling to make the ends of the hot dog round. But the band saw sure gave me a head start. I thanked the teacher for his help and delivered Jon's car to him before I walked home.

Over the next few weeks I worked on my car in the evenings. I chiseled out the ends of the wood so it looked like a hot dog poked out of the bun on both ends. I carved two lines along the length of the top and rounded off the middle section to make it look like a hot dog laying in a bun. Then I sanded and sanded. I wore chunks off my knuckles getting the wood soft and smooth.

I really wanted my car to be a surprise so I painted it at home. I used a light brown paint for the bun, a reddish-orange for the hot dog and yellow for the mustard. I also dipped some sawdust in green paint and scattered it on top to look like relish. A thin line of red paint "ketchup" was the final touch.

Dad helped with the wheels. We spent Thursday evening before the competition adjusting the axles and wheels so they'd be straight and spin freely. After each adjustment, I'd hold the car in the air and test each wheel. "Sorry, Dad," I'd say, "this wheel seems to be rubbing. See how quickly it slows down." And we'd adjust it again. Finally we had it as good as it was going to get.

The next day everyone registered their cars for the race. First the entries were weighed. Any cars that weighed less than the maximum weight were given a piece of lead to tack to the bottom of the car. Cars that were too heavy got a hole drilled in the bottom to lighten them up. That way no one had a weight advantage.

After the weigh-in, the cars were allowed a test run. Each entry had to roll from the top of the track down to the bottom. Afterwards, the cars would be set on a table by the owners' age group. The judges would spend the rest of the afternoon deciding which cars were the best, and choosing runners-up in various categories.

I stood in line with Matt, Dave and Jon, who had pretty

much recovered from his sickness. They kept stroking their cars. Dave's looked immaculate. "It even has a Castrol advertisement and the driver's name alongside the car's number," I said, congratulating him on his work. I thought of the hot dog hidden inside my paper sack.

Dave was fussy about keeping his car unhurt. Matt and Jon were so busy talking about the speed of their vehicles that no one asked what I'd designed.

I let all three of them go ahead of me. When it came my turn, I pulled my car out of the bag. I hadn't cut off as much wood as some of the others, so I only got a small piece of lead to bring my car up to maximum weight. Dave, standing in line for his test run, turned and saw me attaching the lead. "Is that your car, Dean?" he asked.

"Yeah," I answered, not too enthusiastically. I'd been dreading this moment. Now they'd all laugh. I wished I'd made it look like a safari car. Or even like Matt's.

"Hey, that's cool!" Matt said when he saw my hot dog car. "It's really different, Dean."

"Where'd you come up with the idea?" Dave asked. It was obvious he liked it, too.

"Well, it started when my little brother gagged on his hot dog."

Jon took a brief look and nodded. "Is it fast? It's shaped kind of like a bullet. It should be fast." He handed his car to the teacher who was standing on a ladder. He placed Jon's car in the far lane against a movable starting block which poked up through a hole in the bottom of the track. When the race started the blocks in each lane disappeared at once so all the cars got an even start.

Matt and Dave handed their cars over. And then I passed

up my hot dog. Matt's and Jon's cars went the fastest. Mine was about the same speed as Dave's. We picked our cars up where they had stopped against a foam rubber pad at the end of the track. Matt and Jon were excited about how fast their cars had gone. Dave turned his upside-down and studied it with narrowed eyes. Then he whipped out his red Swiss army knife. He pushed up his glasses, held the car at arm's length and squinted. Another adjustment. Another examination. A grunt of satisfaction and he put his car on the table to await judging. Dave's and Jon's were in the ten-year-old category. Mine was for eleven-year-olds. Matt's stood defiant and ugly with the other cars done by twelve-year-olds.

"I'll see you guys this evening at the displays," I said, running home for supper.

Dave and I walked up together after supper and met the other Rhinos. We stood in line to see all the cars on the display tables. By now, the judges had made their decisions and small signs would be standing next to the winning cars. I could tell Dave was excited. He kept pushing his glasses back against his forehead. Matt and Jon didn't care about winning prizes for workmanship or creativity. They joined the Pinewood Derby to race cars down the track.

As the long line snaked its way into the auditorium, we finally saw the cars. From a distance it looked like a yellow card stood next to Dave's car. I whispered to him that he'd won something. Making a fist with his right hand, he pumped his arm up and down and whispered, "Yes!"

Suddenly someone tugged on my arm. I was surprised to see Jill. She looked excited. "Dean, we won!"

I stumbled through the crowd as she dragged me to the table where our cars stood side by side. Her Maasai milk gourd and my hot dog had a yellow card in front reading, "Joint winners — Creative Design Award."

"Isn't that great, Dean!" Jill said, jumping up and down. "We both won." Well, I was excited that I'd won a prize. But the way she carried on made me nervous.

Everyone else in line had stopped to stare at us. My face flushed hot. I looked back at the other Rhinos expecting some support. Instead, Matt and Jon were imitating Jill and pointing at me. Dave smiled, but it was a friendly smile.

"I...uh...I think it's great we both won, Jill. You did a great job. But I think...maybe I shouldn't have cut in line like this."

I pulled away from her and joined the Rhinos. Jill didn't seem to mind. She was flying high.

"I didn't know you worked with Jill," Matt teased. "Are you going to desert the Rhinos now that you've got a girl-friend?"

"She's not my girlfriend!" I hissed, hoping no one had heard Matt. "And we didn't work together."

The line inched ahead until we passed Dave's car. The card next to it said he'd won first place for workmanship. We all pounded him on the back. He deserved the prize. I had hardly seen him since the kits had been handed out.

As we passed by the table where Jill's car stood next to mine, Jon frowned. "Something smells!" he announced, look-ing around. Even when hunting in the forest, Jon seemed to have a stronger sense of smell than the rest of us. He started sniffing until he'd traced the odor. "It's this car of Jill's," he said. He sniffed again. "It really smells smoky, like a Maasai milk gourd!"

"Really?" I leaned over. Jill's car did give off a smoky smell. "That was my idea. I wonder how she did it?"

"Your idea?" Matt asked. "I thought you said you didn't work together."

"We didn't work together. I just said it would be better if it smelled like a real Maasai milk gourd."

"And when did you tell her this?" Jon carried on the teasing. "At one of your planning sessions?"

"I happened to be standing in line next to her when we had our cars cut at the woodshop and we talked for about one minute. We did *not* work together on our cars. I've hardly even seen her since then." I had noticed her in class but I wasn't about to tell the others that!

Dave cut in. "Lay off him, you guys. I think it's pretty cool that he won a prize for his hot dog car." Matt and Jon didn't like it, but they piped down and we filed out of the building.

I woke up early the next morning, got some money from my parents and ran up to school to buy some doughnuts from the senior store. On special days like field days and Pinewood Derby they raised money for a trip at the end of the year called Senior Safari. I bought a dozen and took them home for breakfast. I ate the first one walking the path as the early morning sun filtered through the tall bluegum trees.

After breakfast I went to Dave's house and we walked up to the races. A crowd of people milled around the track. We managed to get good seats in the makeshift grandstand that had been built. Only the contestants whose cars were running in a race could stand next to the track. Everyone else had to watch from the grandstand.

The woodshop teacher tapped on a microphone as Jon and Matt crawled up over the back of the seats and joined us. After telling about the day's schedule the teacher cleared his throat and announced, "Let the Pinewood Derby begin!"

Everyone clapped and cheered. The first group of racers, nine-year-olds, solemnly handed their cars to the starter for the first heat.

chapter eleven

RACING CARS

Half an hour later Jon and Dave raced their cars with the ten-year-olds. They'd been assigned to different groups. Each group would have four races called heats. After each heat, the winner got four points, second place got three points, third place got two points and fourth place got one point. Any car earning ten points or more during the four heats qualified for the finals in the afternoon.

In Jon's first heat his car sailed down in first place. A number four went up next to his name on the wooden scoreboard. Jon's first place finish gave him a great start. His car finished first in the next two heats and third in the final heat, giving him fourteen points and giving him a chance to race in the finals. We cheered and whacked him on the back as he came back and sat with us. Now it was time for Dave's group to race.

Dave examined his car and blew on the wheels once more before he handed it up to the starter. In the first race, Dave's Toyota finished third. Two points. Not very good. He picked the car up from the finish line, and we could see his red knife flashing as he made more changes. His car moved faster in the second race and he finished second. Three more points. In the last race, the rear end of Dave's car fishtailed and it slowed him down in the straightaway. Another car passed his just before the finish line. He had finished third, giving him a total of ten points. Just enough to qualify. But Dave looked worried as he laid his car on its back and began tinkering with it again.

"I barely qualified and if I can't get my car to go faster I'm doomed in the finals," he said when he joined us about ten minutes later.

When it came time for me to race, I found I'd been placed in a group with Jill. "How did you get your car to smell like smoke?" I asked after we'd given our cars to the starter. We walked to the the finish line to await the results of the first heat.

"My mom let me splash liquid smoke on the car just before handing it in for judging."

"Liquid smoke? What's that?"

"Some stuff that comes in a bottle. My mom brings it from the States and uses it on things like hamburgers to make them smell like they've been barbecued."

"They're off!" the announcer said. Looking up at the cars from floor level was so different than in the stands. My wheels hadn't fallen off, my hot dog was rolling straight. But it couldn't keep up with Jill's Maasai milk gourd. It shot like an arrow down the track and won by over five feet. My car came in a respectable second. Two others had crashed on the way down. The results were the same in all four heats. Jill came in first, with sixteen points. My car also qualified with twelve points. I knew I wouldn't have much chance in the finals but I still felt really good. I'd never finished as high as second in a Pinewood Derby race before. And I'd never qualified for the finals. I joined the other Rhinos with a big smile on my face.

"Aren't you going to work on your car to make it go faster?" Dave asked.

"I don't know what else I can do," I said. "I worked on the wheels for a long time with my dad and I can't get them to spin any faster. I think it's just the design of the car. A hot dog just isn't too aerodynamic."

"Try racing it backward in the finals," Dave said. "It won't hurt and, who knows, maybe your car will go faster."

Matt swaggered over to get his car to race in the eleven-year-old heats. He'd won for the past two years and was confident he'd win again. "Come on, Matt," Jon yelled as the starter placed Matt's chunky block-of-wood-on-wheels on the track. Matt's cars all looked alike——just a gradual downhill cut for the front of the car with a square back untouched by anything but a few swabs of paint. Since it had worked for two years, he hadn't made any changes.

We watched the cars drop off the starting blocks. Matt's made the downhill grade and then stopped dead on the track. "What's wrong with Matt's car?" said Jon.

Dave knew at once. "Something's hung up on the

bottom," he said. "See, the wheels are still spinning like crazy, but it's not moving."

Matt had his hands together on top of his head. The stunned look on his face was like my dog when he'd been tied up so he wouldn't follow me to school. Matt ran over and picked up his car. "The nail holding the lead came loose," he said in a loud, complaining voice. He went to the table and one of the teachers helped him tack the lead on securely. But in the second race, almost the same thing happened. This time, the lead stayed on, but the small nail that had been used to tack the lead on dragged on the track.

"Poor Matt," I said. "He can't qualify now."

Matt furiously ripped the lead off the bottom of his car and went to the table. This time they hammered the lead on the top of the car. Now his car looked as if it had been in a wreck where the fender landed on top. His car was fast! It came in first on the last two heats. But the eight points for two first place finishes wasn't enough to qualify for the finals.

"Man, what a rip-off!" Matt said as he slammed into his seat.

None of us answered. We knew how he felt.

"To lose two races because of the lead!" Matt went on. "It wouldn't have been so bad if my car was slow. But did you see those last two races? I had the fastest car on the track and I'd have won first place in the finals for sure."

"Maybe you should have checked how the lead was put on," Dave said gently.

Matt smiled. "I know you're right, Dave. I just don't have time to take care of details like that. Did you see how fast my car went though? Man, I could have won."

As the races went on, Matt got bored. He no longer had a

car in the running so he suggested we go out and play. Since the finals didn't start until 2 P.M. we agreed. We bought hamburgers and Cokes from the seniors. As we sat under a cedar tree, Jill and her friends came up.

"Sorry about your car, Matt," Jill said.

Matt had to impress the girls. "Ah, it was no big deal," he said. I raised my eyebrows when I heard that! "But my car did go fast when I got it fixed, didn't it?" Matt asked, trying to salvage some of his battered pride.

"It was fast, all right," Jill said. "Well, good luck in your races, you guys." She looked at each of us in turn and smiled.

"Thanks," Dave said.

"Yeah," Jon agreed. "And I really liked the smell of your car, Jill. Just like a real Maasai milk gourd."

"That was a great idea," Matt said, nodding.

Jill smiled at me, "Actually, it was Dean who gave me the idea."

The guys all looked at me again with knowing grins. "You sure you didn't work together, Dean?" Matt asked.

"But you're the one who figured out how to do it, Jill," I said, trying to get the attention off of me. "Tell them about the liquid smoke."

The other Rhinos were fascinated that some company sold smoke in a bottle and after the girls left, they talked about that and didn't tease me about Jill.

Matt wasn't too excited about watching the finals, but we persuaded him. "We watched you last year even though none of us qualified," said Dave. "Remember?"

Reluctantly, Matt joined us.

Jon and Dave raced in the ten-year-old final. Despite all Dave's adjustments, he couldn't get his car going fast enough to win. Jon's car never slowed down. It just sped down the track, giving no one else a hope of winning. Somehow Jon had gotten the combination just right: wheels, weight, design. Dave finished a respectable second. He shook Jon's hand after the race. The Rugendo Rhinos had taken first and second place.

My race was next. During the lunch break Dave had used the saw blade of his knife and helped me to file down the car's body near the front wheel to see if that would help it run faster. In the first race, Jill's car rocketed ahead to win. I finished a distant third. I looked up and saw the Rhinos motioning with their hands. They wanted me to race the car backwards. I sighed. Why not? I handed the car up and asked if it could be turned around. The teacher said okay. To my surprise it really sped and I came in second to Jill. I ran back to the starter with my car. "Race it backwards again," I said. This time Jill's car was the slowest lane. The race was close, but the replay video showed that I'd won. I leaped in the air. After three races I had nine points and Jill had eleven. Everything rested on the last race.

We gave our cars to the starter and ran to the finish line to watch. I can still see the final race as if in slow motion. The starting blocks dropped. The cars dived down the steepest part of the track. Down, down, then the beaded cap of Jill's milk gourd crested the small hump first. The cars whizzed down the straightaway. My hot dog was even with Jill's milk gourd. Then it fell behind. I wanted to reach over and pull my car faster, but the race was over. Jill had won by the length of the nose of her car.

I choked back the emotions that wanted to bubble out. I picked up my car and congratulated Jill.

The others comforted me. "Great job, Dean," Matt said. "Too bad you didn't run your car backward in all the races. But still, not a bad haul for the Rhinos this year. Jon got a first for racing. You and Dave got second in the races and trophies for workmanship and creativity. It looks like I'm the only one who didn't win anything this year. But that's okay. I'll still cheer for you guys when you get your awards at the ceremony tonight."

We stayed and watched the older kids and the staff members race.

When I got home in the late afternoon, I could hear voices. I saw some Kenyans standing near the door. I recognized Kamau. *"Ni atia?* Kamau," I said, asking what was going on.

"One of our cows died mysteriously," Kamau said, "and my parents think it has something to do with the curse that Ngugi's father has put on my family. We've come with Pastor Waweru to get your father. The *wazee,* the church elders, think we need to go against the demonic forces and end this attack."

MYSTERIOUS BONES

I went into our house and heard my dad talking with Pastor Waweru. They agreed to go to Ngugi's father as a group of elders. They said they planned to go tomorrow afternoon on Sunday. That would give time for the elders to pray for God's protection and direction.

As Pastor Waweru left with Kamau's family, I asked my dad why they had to go pray again. "Didn't the first prayer work when Jon and Kamau got better? Wasn't that the end of the spiritual battle?"

"The battle goes on all the time, Dean," my dad answered. "In this case, we won a victory when God healed Jon and Kamau. But things aren't yet settled for Ngugi's father. He's still angry and wants to make trouble for Kamau's family. We must get to the root of it."

"Well, I'll pray for you."

"Thanks, Dean, I'll be praying about this, too. Now, I saw your car come in second in the race today. I was proud of you."

"Yeah, that's the closest I've ever come to winning the race. Thanks, Dad, for your help with the wheels. Are you going to watch me get my award at the ceremony tonight?"

"I'll be there, Dean," he said. "Mom and I both will. And I'll bring my camera and get some pictures."

That evening my dad's camera flashed several times, once after Jill and I got the creativity award.

The next day Dad didn't come home after church. Mom said he and the other church elders had decided to fast and pray before going to Ngugi's father. So we ate Sunday dinner without him. Later during the afternoon I stopped several times to pray for Dad and the church elders.

Dad came home in the evening and told us what had happened. He helped me write this part.

After much prayer, the elders had gone to Ngugi's father's home. They didn't accuse him of having a part in the mysterious death of the cow. But Ngugi's father was hostile from the start, and became angrier as they talked and demanded they all leave. Pastor Waweru just stood there asking the others to pray until they got an answer.

Ngugi's father finally calmed down and explained how he'd gone to a famous witch doctor in the nearby town after Ngugi died. The witch doctor told him Ngugi's death was caused by angry spirits. He asked Ngugi's father for a chicken and then said the fault lay with Kamau's family because they no longer poured out offerings to the spirits of their ancestors.

Kamau's grandfather had a strong faith in Christ, so the

spirits couldn't harm Kamau's father. But according to the witch doctor, they could attack Kamau. Unfortunately, Ngugi had been with Kamau. Ngugi died while Kamau survived. Then Ngugi's father wanted revenge for Ngugi's death. And when our prayers stopped that, Ngugi's father had the witch doctor bring a curse on Kamau's family's cattle. "One is dead," Ngugi's father told the elder. "The rest will follow."

My dad said Kamau's father's eyes had popped open in fear. He only owned five cattle, but they were like his savings account. Without cattle, he would have nothing to help his son pay the price to get married.

"What happened then?" I asked.

"Well, we prayed," Dad answered. "It was powerful to see such strong prayers of faith. By the time we had all finished, Ngugi's father was quiet. But I don't think that man is finished."

"What happens next?" I asked.

"Well, we have to keep praying."

Just then Craig popped out of the bathtub. He had a towel wrapped around his waist and was dripping. Dad called for Mom and we read from the Bible and then prayed for Kamau and his family.

"I wish there was some way for Ngugi's father to stop being mad at Kamau's family," I said after our prayer time.

"That would end things," Dad agreed. "But he was still very angry today. We'll have to keep praying that God will change his heart."

As I walked to school with Matt, Jon, and Dave the next morning I was still thinking about Ngugi's death and all the things that had happened since then. "What are you thinking about?" Jon teased. "Jill?"

"No, not her." I explained what had gone on the day before. Jon looked more interested in kicking at pebbles than in my story. Then I said, "I know that when you and Kamau were sick it was some sort of demonic attack. But what about the first sickness where Ngugi died? The witch doctor says it was caused by the spirits. But...I don't know. What if it was caused by something else? If we could find out and prove it, then Ngugi's dad would stop being angry. Suddenly the guys were listening. Jon even stopped kicking the rocks along the path.

"I'm in the mood for a hike in the woods after school today," Matt said. "Why don't we go back to the place where we found Ngugi and Kamau? Maybe we'll find some clue."

The others liked the idea, but I must have looked like a tilapia fish from Lake Naivasha. Matt frowned. "What's the matter, Dean? Don't you want to go?"

"I...I guess I'm just remembering the last time we were there." I told Matt and Jon about how Dave and I had gone back to get tadpoles the day Ngugi died and about the shadows we'd seen.

"Or thought we saw," Dave admitted. "I don't know what it was, but it seemed spooky. I'm not sure I want to go back."

"I'm not sure I want to go there either," Matt said, "but that's the place we'll have to start searching if we're going to uncover any clues. Unless you don't want to go at all."

"I agree, we should go," I said. "But what if I'm wrong? What if the first sickness was caused by demons, too? Would we be in danger by going back there?"

We walked in silence. Suddenly Jill joined us. "What's going on?" she asked. "Usually you guys come past my house talking like crazy."

Matt told her what we'd been talking about.

"Why don't you pray? Ask God to protect you, and help you find out what caused the sickness," she said.

Why hadn't we thought of that? "Yeah," Matt said. "We could pray."

"When are you going?" Jill asked.

"After school," Matt answered.

"I think I'll join you," she said.

"No, I don't think so," said Matt. "It might be too scary for you."

"Try to stop me." She turned, saw a friend, waved, and ran off.

"Great," Matt said, "now we've got your girlfriend coming along."

"She's not my girlfriend!" I said firmly. "How many times do I have to say that?"

We agreed to meet at Matt's house after school so we could sneak away without Jill following us. But as we started down the path, she stepped out from behind a bush and said, "Hi, guys." Then she fell in line behind Dave, who was bringing up the rear.

Matt shrugged his shoulders and led the way. As we came within sight of the pond, Matt slowed down. "Maybe this is a good time to pray," he said.

We quietly prayed and asked God to keep us safe and to help us solve the mystery of Ngugi's death. Silently we approached the area where we'd found Kamau and Ngugi. "Fan out and look for anything that might be useful," Matt said. I noticed Jill stayed close to me. I went behind the short but very bushy tree that shaded the area. Yellow birds hopped in the tree, nibbling at red berries that clustered at the ends of the branches. My dad called the birds yellow-vented bulbuls. We just called them yellow bums. They had black heads, white chests and a big patch of yellow feathers right under their tails. The birds flapped away as we walked near the tree. I got down on one knee and looked around. "I don't see anything," I said.

"Neither do I," Jill answered.

We came back around the tree. Dave returned from searching by the edge of the pond. He was shaking his head.

But Matt and Jon were digging around the blackened place in the grass where the two boys had built their fire. Jon picked up a few things and set them in a pile in the grass. "What did you guys find?" I asked.

"We're not sure," Matt answered. "Jon found some bones. They're almost like chicken bones."

"Chicken bones?" Dave asked. "Don't witch doctors often sacrifice chickens when they contact spirits?"

I felt imaginary creepy crawlies all over my back.

"Maybe," Jon said, "but I think this has nothing to do with the witch doctor. You see this partially burned stick here? It looks like the kind we would use to roast hot dogs on a fire. My guess is that Kamau and Ngugi ate some kind of meat. Cooked it over their fire. And maybe the meat was bad. I don't know. Maybe they found someone's dead chicken and it had died of some sort of disease."

"That could be," Matt said. "I've heard that if an animal dies of some sickness that sounds like ants—"

"Anthrax," said Jill.

"That's right, anthrax," finished Matt. "Anyway, I've heard that if an animal dies of anthrax and anyone eats the meat, they get really sick. It could be something like that."

Jill leaned over. "Look at this bone over here," she said, pointing to a place several yards away. "It still has a chunk of meat on it."

"Let's take it to the hospital," Jon said. "We can have my dad test it to see if there was some sort of disease in the meat."

"And we can ask Kamau what they ate," I said. "That might give us a clue, too."

THE DOROBO HUNTER

We ran up to the hospital. Jon tracked down his dad and told him what we'd found. Dr. Freedman came out and talked to all of us for a few minutes. "I'll take this meat and see what they can find in our lab. There may have been some bacteria in the meat, maybe anthrax, maybe something else. We'll see what shows up under the microscope. But I don't think these are chicken bones. I wonder what they are?"

"Let's go ask Kamau," I said.

We left Dr. Freedman and headed for Kamau's house. He lived on the other side of a small stream where the mission station drew its water. The mission houses had all been built on a flat area where nobody lived. But over the years, many Kenyans had moved from nearby villages to live right next to the compound. Some families had come years before to go to school or to find work. Others had moved down from villages up in the hills as families grew and plots of land could no longer be divided for each of the adult sons. A sizable new town had grown up on the other side of the river with shops, *chai* houses, as well as the homes and small farms.

"Who knows which house is Kamau's?" asked Matt.

"I do," said Dave. "His dad is a *fundi,* a carpenter, and he works with my dad. Sometimes my dad gives him a ride home after work. It's not too far."

At Kamau's, we saw a sheep tethered to a stake. It ripped up grass and looked up at us. Kamau came out from the separate cookhouse carrying an empty plastic jug. Once a white container for oil, the jug now was a dirty brown. "I was just going down to the river to fetch water," he said.

We offered to help. He gave us each a one-gallon jug and we walked down the steep path. "We've been wondering," Matt began, "if you and Ngugi ate any meat the day you got sick. Like a chicken or something."

"Why do you ask?" Kamau looked puzzled.

"We thought maybe you got sick from eating meat from a sick bird or animal."

"You don't think our sickness that day was caused by the spirits?" he asked.

"We're not sure," I said. "When both you and Jon almost died, we know that sickness was caused by evil spirits. But what if the first sickness wasn't caused by spirits? Then we could show Ngugi's father and he'd stop having the witch doctor put curses on you and your family."

We'd reached the river and were holding the jugs under the water to let them fill up.

"Maybe you're right," Kamau said. "But I know the meat

wasn't bad. It was a rabbit. Ngugi and I had killed it with a club that morning. It was healthy. And the meat was very sweet. No, I don't think it could have been the meat. I still don't know. I think it was the spirits that made us get sick."

We hauled the water back up to Kamau's house, thanked him for his help and left. "Well, we know what kind of meat it was," Matt said. "Rabbit."

We went back to the hospital. Dr. Freedman told us they wouldn't have results on the test until the next day. The shadows had lengthened. We said good-bye and headed for home. I walked Jill part way to her house.

The next day after lunch Jon joined us while Matt and I kicked a soccer ball around the field. "My dad said the lab finished examining the meat. They couldn't find anything that would have made Kamau and Ngugi sick. No poison in the meat. Nothing at all."

The first bell rang for school. "We need to decide what to do next," Matt said. "Let's meet at our clubhouse in the *mugumo* tree after school at four o'clock. That will give me enough time to go home after school and have a snack. Jon, you're in the same class with Dave. Can you pass the message on to him?"

After school, we gathered at our tree fort and discussed everything we knew. "Well," Matt concluded, "it doesn't look like we've made any progress to find out what caused Ngugi's death. Maybe it *was* a spiritual attack."

Jon sat up, suddenly alert. He moved to one of the small windows we'd cut out of the wall. "Look down there!" he whispered. We all crowded by the window.

A small brown man crouched, partially hidden behind a bush. He peered ahead into the ravine below. Then, like an escaped shadow, he slipped away from his hiding place. We could see he wore a brown cloth tied toga-style over his shoulder. A large knife in a leather sheath was strapped to his waist. A wooden quiver of arrows hung on a leather strap over his back. And he carried a bow. An arrow was poised for release as he eased his way forward.

"Hey, who are you and what are you doing?" shouted Matt.

In that instant a thrashing sound filled the ravine and a bushbuck exploded out of the thick brush, sprinting for safety. The small man looked up to see who had interrupted his hunt. He shook his bow angrily at us and then disappeared, melting into the shadows of the forest.

"That guy was different," Matt said.

"I wish you hadn't shouted," Jon said. "I would have liked to see if he hit that bushbuck. Man, how did he even know the bushbuck was there? I didn't see a thing."

Matt defended himself. "I couldn't see any bushbuck either. For all I knew he might have been planning to shoot a person. So I called out."

"Let's go look around," Jon said.

We clambered down out of our tree fort. But not even Jon's tracking skills could find a trace of the mysterious little hunter. We went home, not sure what to do next besides keeping up our prayers for Kamau's family.

That night I asked my dad about the hunter we'd seen in the forest. He listened with interest and started nodding. "He was probably a Dorobo," my dad said.

"What's a Dorobo?" I asked.

"Well," he explained, "they are a small tribe that lives by hunting and collecting honey in the forests. I've only met a few, but small groups of them live in most of the thick forest areas of Kenya."

"Can you tell me more?" I liked collecting knowledge about the different tribes that lived in Africa.

"From what I've gathered, they lived here before the other tribes. As the Maasai, Kikuyu and Kalenjin moved into this area from the north, the Dorobo moved away. Actually, the proper name for the tribe is Okiek. But most people call them Dorobo which comes from the Maasai word for the tribe—*Iltorrobo*—which means poor people or people without cows."

"Why have we never seen any before if they live in our forest?" I asked.

"Well, the Dorobo are very shy and secretive. But I doubt there's a group living in our forest or I'm sure we'd have heard about them. Our forest isn't that large, you know. Just the three or four miles between here and the plains. The man you saw might just be passing through looking for animals to hunt. Actually the Dorobo did live near here years ago. The Kikuyu called them the Athi, the pioneers. But as the Kikuyu moved in and started farming, the Dorobo traded their forest land for beehives."

"They did what?"

My dad laughed. "Traded their forest for beehives. You see, the Dorobo love honey more than anything. They love to eat it raw, right from the honeycomb. But until the Kikuyu arrived, the Dorobo had to search hard to find honey in trees with holes or in small cracks in rock cliffs. They would follow a bird called the honey guide which would show them where honey was in return for a share in the honey. Or they'd follow the bees themselves. But it was a hit-or-miss business.

"Then the Dorobo learned that the Kikuyu had invented a portable beehive from logs that were split in half. The Kikuyu hollowed out the middle and tied the two halves back together again using vines. They dangled the log beehive from any tree they wanted and checked it from time to time to see if they had any bees coming in to make honey."

"So the Dorobo traded their land for beehives," I finished.

"Yes. In those days there was plenty of forest and the Dorobo continually ranged from place to place anyway. So they didn't think they were giving up much. And in exchange, they got beehives and could find honey with a lot less effort."

"I guess it was a good trade."

"Yes, until recently," my dad said. "With so many people here in Kenya, the farming tribes like the Kikuyu and Kipsigis have cut down a lot of trees to grow crops. So the Dorobo that remain are being pushed farther and farther into what's left of the forest."

"How do you know all this stuff?" I asked.

"I've done some study with Mr. Njogu, the Kenyan editor at our magazine. We did a series on different tribes in some recent articles."

All the talk about Dorobo and hunting reminded me about our genet cat trap. With all our excitement about the spiritual warfare and the Pinewood Derby, we hadn't been checking it regularly. I decided I would wake up early the next morning and have a look.

My alarm clock woke me up in the usual way, clanking until I hammered down the button. Then I turned on my light to see what time it was. 6 A.M. I yawned, got up and dressed, dragging on an old sweatshirt over my school clothes to ward off the damp, early-morning cold.

I looked around in the kitchen for some new bait for the trap. My dad hadn't been fishing recently so I had no fish heads. I finally grabbed a piece of bread and stuck it in my pocket. At the door I put on an old pair of boots. With dew on the grass and bushes it would be wet and I didn't want to ruin my new tennis shoes. With all the dirt around Rugendo, they already had an orange-brown tint to them. But if I didn't get them wet they would last longer.

I slid down parts of the trail as I hurried to the place where we'd set the trap. The soft rattling burp of colobus monkeys echoed through the ravines. I slowed down to catch my breath when suddenly a big brown francolin bird ran out from behind a bush, flapping and screeching wildly. My heart was beating like a machine gun, and I knew why the Kikuyu people called francolins "birds that scare grown men."

I finally arrived at the tree where our trap was hidden. Reaching down carefully, I pushed aside the bushes. The trap was still set. Nothing had disturbed it and the peanut butter on the stick had turned gray with mold. I really didn't want to touch the moldy peanut butter so I laid the bread on the stick and gave it a squeeze with my hand. The bread stuck around the peanut butter. I pushed the trap back into its hiding place. I'd tell the other guys and we'd have to put some proper bait in the trap.

As I stood up I noticed a quick flicker of motion to my right.

chapter fourteen

HUNTING WITH POISON ARROWS

I nearly leaped out of my boots. The same little brown man with the bow and arrow slipped out from behind a tree. My throat was too dry to scream. I wanted to run but my legs felt heavy, as if there were huge clumps of mud clinging to my shoes.

Then the man smiled. I felt myself take a breath, but I looked around, hoping he'd leave so I could escape. Instead he motioned at the bush where I'd just hidden the trap. I looked slowly down at the bush and then back to the little man. Then I pointed at the bush with a frown on my face. He nodded and squatted down, pointing again.

I tried some Swahili. *"Unataka nini?"* I asked. "What do you want?"

"*Kuona mtego,*" he replied.

He had answered back in Swahili. At least we could communicate a little, but I didn't know Swahili too well. He had said he wanted to see something. I didn't know what *mtego* meant, but I assumed it must mean our trap. So I reached under the bush and dragged it out.

In an instant the man had crouched down and gingerly touched the trap. He felt around the corners, pursing his lips and nodding seriously. Putting his head upside down like a flamingo dredging for food, he peered into the box. He reached in and tugged on the bait stick. The door fell on his arm.

He jumped back, jerking his arm out of the box. Then he examined the wires and pulley that let the door drop down, and gave an approving grunt. Bending over again, he lifted the door and unwired the bait stick. The man stood up holding the stick with the moldy peanut butter and bread crumpled around it. He sniffed it, then wrinkled his nose and grimaced. He flung the stick into the woods in obvious disgust, saying words I didn't understand.

"Yeah, it smells kind of bad," I muttered. "No wonder we didn't catch anything in our trap."

He looked at me questioningly. I tried to explain in Swahili but failed.

The man then stepped behind the tree. I thought he would disappear again. But he popped back again holding the limp body of a dead blue monkey.

"*Tumpili,*" he said, the Swahili name for the monkey. He pulled out a knife so big it was almost a small sword from a leather sheath tied to a rawhide thong around his waist. The blade was about a foot long and it looked razor sharp. He swung at a nearby bush, lopping off a branch with one swing. I cringed a bit. What was he doing?

Holding the branch, he stripped off the bark and cut a stick about the same size as the bait stick he'd thrown away. With a few deft strokes of his knife he cut off a small strip of monkey meat. He stabbed the sharp end of the stick through the meat and then wrapped the meat around the stick several times, tying it like a shoelace.

Dropping to his knees, he reached into our trap and attached the new bait stick to the trip wire. I showed him how to set the door of the trap. The man pushed the box back under the bush. Using the dead monkey as a broom he swept over the area leading to the trap. Then, draping the monkey over his shoulder, the hunter motioned for me to move away. I followed him up the path. He stopped and pointed back at the trap and told me in Swahili that we would catch something by the next morning.

I thanked him and asked him if he was a Dorobo. "*Ndiyo*," he answered. "It is so."

I told him I had learned from my dad how his people were famous hunters. The man smiled.

"Can you show me and my friends how you hunt?" I asked. He agreed to meet us after school at our tree fort. "The place where we interrupted your hunt yesterday," I said. "Do you know time? Can you be there at 4 P.M.?"

He lifted up his arm to display a digital watch. He told me he'd traded some honey for the watch at the market.

I told him I had to go to school and we'd meet later. He held out his hand in farewell and told me his name. "I am Kosen," he said.

"And I'm Dean." We shook hands briefly. I started up the

hill. When I turned to wave good-bye, he had already slipped into the forest. I ran most of the way back home, stopping only twice because I had a side ache. I stopped by the house, tore off my boots and grabbed a piece of toast to eat on the way to school.

"Did you catch anything in your trap?" my dad asked.

"No," I answered, "but we will tomorrow."

He raised his eyebrows and set down his coffee cup. "What makes you so sure?"

"Remember that Dorobo guy we saw in the forest yesterday? Well, this morning he met me at the trap and he helped me to set it with a piece of monkey meat for bait. And this afternoon he's agreed to take us hunting and show us how he tracks animals and things. I can't wait to tell the other Rhinos."

"Sounds like fun. I'd like to come along, but I'm going to Nairobi today to interview a pastor who grew up in a home with two mothers."

"Two mothers?" I asked, my question spilling out around the peanut butter and jam toast I had just stuffed into my mouth.

"We're doing a magazine on polygamy," he explained. "That's when a man marries more than one wife. We're interviewing a pastor who grew up in this way. Anyway, when I get back tonight I want to hear how the hunting trip went."

I waved good-bye and hurried out the door. In the distance I could hear the first bell ringing at school. If I ran, I could just get there before the last bell rang.

At recess I went to the water fountain first. The peanut butter had left a stale taste in my mouth, and since I'd eaten most of it running up the hill I hadn't brushed my teeth. I sloshed a big gulp of water around in my mouth, spit it out on a nearby banana plant and went looking for Matt.

I found him on the soccer field. He told me to join his team. While the other players argued about who would play where, I told Matt about the Dorobo man agreeing to take us hunting after school. Matt was so excited he couldn't concentrate on the soccer game and fluffed two easy chances to score.

We all met at Matt's after school and jogged down to our tree fort together. We looked around but couldn't see Kosen, the Dorobo hunter, anywhere. Matt blamed me right away. "I hope you didn't mess things up, Dean," he said. "Maybe when you were talking to him in Swahili you mixed up the day or the time. Or maybe he said he wouldn't come and you thought he meant he would come."

"I thought he said he'd meet us here today at four. You know how Africans start counting the hours at the beginning of the day so seven in the morning is *saa moja* or the first hour. I told him we'd meet at the tenth hour and that's four o'clock, isn't it?"

"We also have to remember that this is Africa," Dave said. "Even if the guy did agree to meet us at this time, he may be late. I've gone to weddings scheduled for ten in the morning that didn't start until late afternoon. He could be very late."

Just then we heard a snort of laughter and Kosen appeared. He'd been standing next to a tree about ten yards away. But until he laughed we hadn't seen him. With his soft brown blanket and his copper-tone skin he'd blended into the background.

"*Twende.* Let's go," he said in greeting and strode into the forest. We followed him without saying a word, Jon right on his heels. I let Dave and Matt go ahead of me. Even when we Rhinos stalked pigeons Jon and Matt always chided me for making too much noise. I didn't want to annoy the Dorobo hunter. I picked my way carefully through the bushes and dead branches on the ground.

Today I was determined not to make any noise. So I kept my eyes focused on the path in front of me. That's why I didn't notice the others had already stopped until I bumped into Dave who had crouched down to watch. He almost fell over, but caught his balance with one hand. His face told me he didn't appreciate my bump. I started to say I was sorry when Matt turned and drew a line across his neck with his index finger to keep quiet. I crouched like the others and watched Kosen.

His shoulders leaned forward and he stood perfectly still, peering into the forest. I tried to follow his gaze but could only see rippling shadows under the thick canopy of trees. After a few minutes that seemed to last an hour, he signaled for us to follow. He made no sound as he crept forward. Unlike me, Kosen didn't pay any attention to where he stepped. He looked ahead. But as he stepped, his feet seemed to touch the ground and then gently draw up as if on a cushion. He glided ahead of us. I let Dave get several steps ahead of me before I followed.

Our line came to a halt again. The Dorobo motioned us to come closer. He pointed to the ground and said a large bushbuck had passed by in the past two minutes.

"How can you tell?" asked Matt. Kosen said the shape of the print told him it was a bushbuck, not some other animal. The depth of the print in the ground told him how heavy the animal was. And because a blade of grass that had been stepped on still smelled a certain way, it meant the animal had passed by recently. Jon nodded excitedly. I was still trying to see the footprint in the thick layer of dead leaves.

We worked our way through the thick forest for another ten minutes and arrived at the edge of a small clearing. Kosen had already lined up his arrow on the taut bowstring by the time I knelt down next to the others. Ever so slightly he drew back the bowstring, gripping the shabby looking feathers on the end of his arrow. I couldn't even see what he was aiming at, but we all held our breath and watched.

The bow bent as the string stretched. Briefly, he held that position then released the arrow. The arrow hummed with a soft whirring as it disappeared. At the same instant a bush-buck gave a startled bark and leaped out from where he'd been browsing across the glade. The arrow was stuck in the animal's shoulder. But it fell out as the buck rushed away. With a big smile, Kosen ran into the clearing and picked up his arrow.

"Looks like he didn't get much power into his shot," Matt said. "It was a fun stalk, but I'm a bit disappointed. I thought he'd make a kill."

Kosen picked up the arrow and very carefully wrapped the metal arrowhead with a long strip of softened leather. He made sure he didn't touch it. The arrowhead, shaped like a small knife blade, had no barbs.

Matt asked him why he wrapped the arrow so carefully.

Kosen said one word. *"Sumu."* It meant poison.

"You used a poison arrow?" Matt asked.

Kosen nodded and found a spot of red liquid in the grass. *"Damu,"* he said. Blood. And he started following the trail.

Within a hundred yards we found the bushbuck. It was dead.

As Kosen began cutting up the meat, we asked him about the poison arrow. It got too complicated for me, but Matt explained that the poison somehow made the animal bleed to death internally without poisoning the meat.

"He says he uses that arrowhead especially for animals this size. The head is sharp enough to penetrate the skin and insert the poison, but it usually falls out easily. That way he doesn't bend the arrowhead and can use it again. He also says the poison is so strong that if you nick yourself with a poison-tipped arrow you'll be dead within minutes. That's why he wrapped it so carefully."

Matt asked Kosen how he made the poison. He looked thoughtful. Then he said he could show us how he made the poison but it was too late now. He pointed to the sky. We could see the dull orange of the setting sun. He smiled and gave us a leg of the bushbuck to take home.

Matt arranged for us to meet Kosen at the tree fort again on Saturday morning so he could show us how he made his poison.

Then Kosen hoisted the rest of the meat and disappeared.

chapter fifteen

THE POISON
ARROW TREE

We chattered like vervet monkeys as we hustled to get home before dark. "Did you see how fast the poison worked? Did you see how silently he walked through the bush? Did any of you see what he was shooting at?" The questions flew back and forth without many answers.

At home I told my dad about the hunting trip and the poison arrow. He listened with interest. And when I told him we'd be going to see how he made the poison on Saturday he insisted on joining us. I wasn't sure what the other guys would think of my dad tagging along.

I told them the next morning at school. Jon said his dad wanted to come too. As a doctor he wanted to see how this type of poison was made.

"I really didn't want him to come," Jon said, "but if your dad is coming too, I guess it won't be so bad."

"I just thought of something," I said, changing the subject. "The Dorobo man promised we'd have a genet cat in our trap this morning."

"We'll have to check it right after school this afternoon," Matt said.

When we arrived at the trap we heard a thumping sound. We pulled the box out and saw a genet cat, banging against the sides, trying to get out.

"I can't believe it!" Matt said. "We caught one."

"Yeah," Jon said. "Look at the beautiful black spots on his back."

"Let's take him home," I suggested. "Then my dad can take some pictures."

We took turns carrying home the trap. My dad was happy to take some pictures. We released the genet cat into a small chicken wire pen we'd built to keep our puppies out of trouble. It darted back and forth inside the wire. Dad couldn't get it to stop long enough to get any decent pictures. Then, before we could do anything to stop it, the cat found a small gap in the fence and escaped into the woods.

Jon was the only one who was really upset. "I wanted that skin," he said, miffed that our catch had gotten away.

Matt consoled him. "We caught one so I'm sure we can get another one later."

For now, our attention shifted from trapping to learning how the Dorobo made poison.

We all walked together to our tree fort on Saturday morning. Again, we didn't see Kosen and then, suddenly, he was there smiling. My dad and Dr. Freedman greeted him and they spent a few minutes exchanging news.

"He says he doesn't live around here," my dad translated. "His family lives about thirty miles away in a forest called Olpusimoru. But he came over here for a few weeks to see what it's like. Farmers are buying up some of the forest land by their home and as they cut down the trees and start planting potatoes and corn, it's harder to find honey. He's looking for a better place to live."

"What does he think of our forest?" I asked.

"He likes it. But it isn't large enough to support a family for very long. He wants to set up a few beehives. He could harvest them once or twice a year even if he still lives in the Olpusimoru forest. He says there aren't enough animals to hunt here often."

Jon's dad said he was a doctor and wanted to know about the poison. My dad asked if he could take some pictures. Kosen smiled and led our parade through the forest.

We hiked down the hills. Sunshine filtered through to us as the forest thinned. Then Kosen stopped beside a stubby tree with branches covered with small leaves and a few red berries.

He told us this was the tree where he got his poison. He chipped off small pieces of bark with his knife and put them in a battered, smoke-blackened pot. Then he asked if any of us had brought matches. We hadn't. He shrugged and pulled out a flat piece of wood with a blackened hole in its center and a smooth hand-worn stick.

Kosen got down on his knees and gathered a small pile of tiny twigs and dried grass. Then he set his fire-starter on the ground with the stick in the hole. He placed twigs and grass around the hole and rubbed his hands back and forth. The stick twirled in the hole and soon the straw began to smoke and glow. He blew gently on the sparks. Within a few minutes he had a good fire crackling.

He said he needed more firewood so we gathered enough sticks to keep the fire going. Once it had burned into glowing coals, he set his pot of tree bark on the fire and stepped back. He said the bark had to cook down into an orange-colored liquid and then simmer for the rest of the morning before it would become arrow poison.

Jon's dad had a lot of questions as to how the poison worked. Kosen explained how it made the animal bleed inside and how it didn't harm the meat. Dr. Freedman examined the leaves, trying to identify what family of tree it belonged to.

Kosen watched Jon's dad curiously. But when Jon's dad started to bend a branch to break it off, the Dorobo quickly told him to stop.

"Why? What's wrong?" Jon's dad asked.

Kosen told him the tree's poison could be harmful in other ways and he didn't want anyone to be hurt.

"What other ways?" my dad asked. "The berries don't seem to be toxic. The birds are eating them."

"The berries don't bother birds," Kosen said, "but they are dangerous to people. Never eat them. And the branches can make a person very sick."

"How?" asked Jon's dad.

"If you cook meat over a fire made of the branches or use the branches as skewers for your meat it can make you very sick. Somehow the poison moves from the smoke or the sticks themselves into the meat. I don't know how it works.

But we Dorobo are very careful around these trees."

Jon piped up. "I don't know if it means anything, but there's a poison arrow tree right next to the place where Ngugi died."

His dad turned quickly. "There is? Why didn't you tell us before?"

"I didn't know it was a poison arrow tree until this morning when the hunter told us. But I'm sure there's a tree identical to this one over by the pond."

The rest of us Rhinos agreed. "You're right, Jon," I said. "That tree is just like this one. Do you think it might be why Ngugi died?"

"I think we should go over there right now and find out," Dr. Freedman said. He and my dad talked with the Dorobo and explained about the two boys getting sick and Ngugi's death. Taking his pot of poison off the fire, Kosen hid it and stamped out the fire, and we headed for the pond.

When we arrived Jon's dad went straight to the tree and looked closely. "It sure is the same species," he said. Kosen grunted in agreement. "Yes, this is a poison arrow tree," he said. "I passed it some weeks back."

I looked at Dave and whispered, "The shadow we saw the day Ngugi died." Dave nodded.

Kosen bent over the blackened grass where the boys had cooked their rabbit. Sifting through the remains of the small fire, he picked up some sticks and shook his head sadly. "It looks like the boys cooked their rabbit over branches from the poison arrow tree." He pointed at a tiny bit of charred rabbit meat on one stick. "And one of the boys used a green branch to spear his meat and hold it over the fire. I'm sure that's why he died."

"Poisoned by the poison arrow tree," my dad mused. "Now this puts a different light on these spiritual attacks that are continuing against Kamau's family. We'd better go over and talk to them right away."

"Wait a minute," Dr. Freedman said. "What about all that spiritual warfare stuff when Kamau got sick the second time and then Jon almost died? Was that also caused by the poison arrow tree?"

"No," my dad said. "That was definitely a spiritual attack brought on by the witch doctor. We weren't prepared and some of our gossiping and anger over cultures clashing had given Satan a foothold and left us open to attack. What this means, though, is that Ngugi's death was not caused by any spiritual forces. It didn't happen—as the witch doctor and Ngugi's father say—because Kamau's family angered the spirits. Ngugi died because he cooked his meat on a stick from this tree. If we explain that to Kamau's family and then share this with Ngugi's family, we may be able to stop Ngugi's father from bringing more curses on Kamau's family."

My dad felt it was important to talk to the two families as soon as possible. He and Jon's dad went off to find Pastor Waweru and the church elders. Kosen went with them to explain about the poison arrow tree.

We walked to Matt's house. "Let's get something to drink," Matt said. "My mom was going to bake cookies this morning."

We walked into a comforting blanket of warm cookie aroma at Matt's house. We sat down on the couch as Matt pulled some cold Cokes from the fridge.

"Looks like we got to the bottom of the mystery," Matt said, as we drank Cokes and ate peanut butter cookies.

"Yeah, a poison arrow tree," said Jon. "I wonder if we

could brew up our own pot of poison? The recipe didn't look that hard."

"No way," said Dave. "That stuff is scary. It can kill. I'm not sure I want to eat pigeons any more. What if they'd been eating the berries?"

We laughed. "It's potent poison," Matt said, "but not that dangerous, Dave. Besides, for some reason it doesn't affect birds. That's another mystery."

"Well, I'm definitely not going to try to solve that mystery," Dave said firmly.

My dad came home at supper time. He sat down and let out a sigh that sounded like a leaky air mattress. But he looked happy.

"What happened?" I asked.

"We went to Kamau's family first," he said. "Kamau said that they had cooked their rabbit on a fire and some of their firewood had come from under the tree. And Ngugi had used a green branch from the poison arrow tree as his cooking stick. Kamau said he'd cut a stick from a different tree. That explains why Ngugi died and Kamau survived. Dr. Freedman did a bit of research from a botany book while we waited for Pastor Waweru. According to the book, the poison arrow tree produces an anti-coagulant poison that is undetectable."

"What's that anti-whatever you said?" I asked.

"Anti-coagulant means it stops the blood from clotting so the victim bleeds to death inside very quickly. Just like the Dorobo said. But the poison is untraceable. That's why the lab found nothing when the boys were sick. Even the meat you found by their fire showed no trace of poison."

"What did Kamau's family say when they found out it was poison and not some ancestral spirits?" I asked.

"They wanted us to go with them to tell Ngugi's father. Pastor Waweru told them they first had to be willing to forgive Ngugi's father. Kamau's family had a hard time with this at first. He was angry with Ngugi's father for bringing the sickness that almost killed Kamau. And now he'd lost a cow. But Pastor Waweru made it clear that unless Kamau's family was willing to forgive Ngugi's family they would still be open to spiritual attack.

"Kamau surprised them by getting on his knees and praying first. He asked God to forgive him for being angry with Ngugi's father. When his parents saw him they soon followed. It was special to see God working in the hearts of Kamau's family.

"Then we went as a team to Ngugi's family. We explained about the poison arrow tree and the cause of Ngugi's death. But Ngugi's father was still hard. He said he didn't know if he believed this story. Then Kosen explained about the poison. Ngugi's father still wanted revenge for Ngugi's death. But when Kamau and his parents said they had confessed their own anger and wanted to forgive him for bringing the sickness on Kamau and their cow, it really impressed him. Then Dr. Freedman, tears in his eyes, said that he had been angry at Ngugi's father because of the curse on Jon. But he prayed right there and asked Ngugi's father to forgive him.

"Well, Ngugi's father visibly trembled. He said he couldn't believe we were forgiving him after what he'd done. Pastor Waweru said we had to forgive others because Christ had forgiven us.

"Ngugi's father sat down on a wooden chair outside his house and asked us to pray for him. 'I need to know Jesus,' he said. 'I've seen his power over Satan as you stopped the attack on Kamau and Jon. But now I see the power of for-giveness. I know I must follow the Master.' Pastor Waweru led him in a short prayer and Ngugi's father and mother both accepted Christ as their Savior."

"That's amazing," I said.

"God is always amazing when we put our full trust in him," my dad said. "And listen to this. Kosen said he wanted to know more about Jesus, too. He's invited us to visit his village next Sunday and tell them about the Word of God."

"That's great, Dad! What an end to our mystery."

"Not an end, Dean," he said, putting his arm around my shoulder. "The battle against Satan and his kingdom goes on. We always need to be prepared and ready to fight. And when we pray and put everything in God's hands, the victory is ours, in Jesus' name. Come on, let's go have some supper."

THE END

GLOSSARY

1. *Bushbuck* — A small antelope that lives in forest thickets and dense bush. The bushbuck is mostly chestnut brown with white stripes and spots, about three feet high at the shoulder and has foot-long horns. It is shy and elusive, moving mostly at night. Its voice is a loud clear bark.

2. *Genet cat* (JEN-net) — Not really a cat at all, the genet is a small weasel-like carnivore with skin similar to a leopard's, tan and covered with spots. It has a long tail with black rings. A genet cat weighs about five pounds and has short legs and a long body (one to two feet long not counting the tail). It hunts at night.

3. *Francolin* (FRANK-oh-lin) — A family of chicken-like birds, they come in various shades of brown. Francolins

usually spend most of their time on the ground looking for food. When surprised they will fly into the sky with a shrill call.

4. *Colobus monkey* (CULL-uh-bus) — A black-and-white monkey that lives in the trees. It has white whiskers and beard surrounding a jet black face. The hair on the colobus monkey's shoulders is white and flowing like a cape. The colobus doesn't have a thumb and only has four fingers on each hand. Early in the morning colobus monkeys make a low gurgling sound that can be heard for a long distance.

5. *Vervet monkey* (VER-vet) — A medium-sized monkey, part of the green monkey family. It has a dark face and white whiskers, and is light grey or olive green on the back with a white stomach. It has a long stiff tail and black feet.

6. *Tilapia fish* (Till-AH-pee-uh) — A freshwater food fish resembling an American sunfish. Tilapia are shiny grey in color with large round scales. They normally don't bite on a lure and are usually caught in nets.

7. *Mandazi* (Muh-NDAH-zee) — The Swahili word for square African doughnuts without a hole in the middle. *Mandazi* are often served with tea for dunking.

8. *Chai* (CHAH-ee [said almost as one syllable]) — The word for tea in Swahili. *Chai* is made by boiling a mixture of milk and water in a pan over a fire. When it begins to boil tea leaves and sugar are mixed in and the *chai* is set aside for a few minutes. The *chai* is then poured through a strainer. It is sweet and milky and, if cooked over a traditional cook fire, it has a smoky taste as well.

9. *Mugumo tree* (Moo-GOO-mo) — *Mugumo* is a Kikuyu word for a wild fig tree that grows to immense size. It was considered the sacred home of ancestral spirits by the Kikuyu

people. They often were used for traditional sacrifices and worship.

10. *Mganga* (Mm-GAH-nguh) — The Swahili word for a traditional healer or witch doctor. These men often used various herbs and bark from the forest to make curative medicine. But they also made contact with evil spirits in their attempts to find the cause of someone's sickness. They also were called in to put curses on enemies.

11. *Fundi* (FOO-ndee) — The Swahili word for a skilled craftsman or builder. A carpenter, a bricklayer and a mechanic all are people who would be called a *fundi*.